PARTY RECIPES

PARTY RECIPES

By
SYLLA J. BHAISA

JAICO PUBLISHING HOUSE
Mumbai ● Delhi ● Bangalore
Kolkata ● Hyderabad ● Chennai

PARTY RECIPES
ISBN 81-7224-233-6

First Jaico Impression : 1978
Seventh Jaico Impression : 1997
Eighth Jaico Impression : 2002

Published by:
Jaico Publishing House
121, Mahatma Gandhi Road
Mumbai - 400 001.

Printed by:
R.N. Kothari
Sanman & Co.
113, Shivshakti Ind. Estate,
Marol Naka, Andheri (E),
Mumbai - 400 059.

CONTENTS

CONTENTS

FOREWORD

This book has been written at the request of my family and friends. I learnt the basic tenets of cooking at a cooking class, which I attended for six months after finishing my schooling. After that, I have learnt by trial and error. Of course, in those days one could afford to try out new recipes, and if they did not come out well, one could always try again, thanks to my mother, who always encouraged me and appreciated my effort. However, in these days of shortages and with food being so expensive, it is not always easy, so every recipe has been tried, tested and perfected by me with an experience of over forty years.

There are simple as well as exotic dishes catering to our Indian palate and over 90% of the ingredients are available all over India. I'm sure this book will come in handy for entertaining at home, which most people do these days. A few dishes made at home will always be more appreciated than anything bought outside. I have not given any fancy names to the recipes—each name signifies what it contains.

My thanks are due to my family, without whose criticism, help and encouragement this book would not have been possible.

If there are any questions regarding these recipes, I will be very happy to answer them through letters addressed to my publishers.

Wishing you all Bon Appetit,

SYLLA J. BHAISA

GLOSSARY

A LA MODE:	Pies or cakes, served with a scoop of icecream.
A LA KING:	Chicken boned and served in rich cream sauce with mushrooms, pimento, and flavoured with sherry.
BAIN MARIE:	To cook in a double boiler, or over a pan of simmering water, just below boiling point.
BLANCH:	Dipping it in hot water for a few minutes, and then draining off the water and peeling the skin off.
BOUQUET GARNI:	A bunch of parsley, bay leaf and thyme leaf, mostly used for soups and gravies.
BLANQUETTE:	White sauce made with cream and egg yolks and used to cover chicken or veal dishes, and garnished with small onions and mushrooms.
BAKE:	To cook in the oven.
BASTE:	To pour pan gravy over food roasting in the oven or any other liquid marinade.
BISQUE:	A rich cream soup made from chicken, fish, shell fish, or vegetables.
BLEND:	Mix ingredients thoroughly by hand or blend in a liquidiser.
BOMB:	Moulded icecream or mousse frozen.
BUTTER CLARIFIED:	Gently heat butter over low heat, let it stand for a while, then strain the clear yellow oil, leaving the sediments.

CAPON:	Young cockerel.
CARAMELIZE:	To heat sugar in a heavy pan until melted and golden brown. Used for custards and sauces, also for flavouring cakes and puddings.
CASSEROL:	Food cooked in a covered earthenware dish or pyrex dish.
CAVIER:	Salted roe of sturgeon, used for canapes, appetizers.
CHANTILLY:	Sweetened and flavoured cream, used in pastry, eclairs, and meringues.
CHOWDER:	A thick soup, made with chicken, fish, vegetables, corn.
CONDIMENTS:	Seasonings such as salt, pepper, cayenne, herbs and spices.
COMPOT:	Stewed fruits, served chilled in individual glasses.
COURT BOUILLON:	Fish stock made from odd bits of fish, used in fish dishes such as "Sole Bonne Femme".
CREPES:	Thin pancakes used for sweet or savoury fillings or for making "Crepes Suzettes".
CRACKLING:	Rind of pork, fried very crisp.
CROQUETTS:	Mixture of ground meats or fish, bound by white sauce seasoned, dipped in beaten egg and breadcrumbs and fried in deep oil.
CROUTONS:	Cubes of bread fried or toasted, and served with soups.
DOUGH:	Mixture of butter or fat, flour and liquid along with any other ingredients as for making pastry, breads, cakes and biscuits.
DEVILLED:	Highly seasoned foods.
DREDGE:	To coat with flour, sugar or sprinkle sugar over cakes

DRIPPING: Oil or fat left in the pan with a little gravy after the food is cooked.

FRICASSE: Dish made with chicken in white sauce.

FLOUR: Plain or self-raising, use plain, unless otherwise specified.

FLAKE: To separate in thin slices.

FLAMBE: To pour spirits on food and igniting it at the table, or even whilst cooking.

FORCEMEAT: Paste of fish or meats, used for stuffing.

FRY: To cook in deep oil or fat.

GOULASH: Beef stew made with paprika flavour.

GIBLETS: Odd pieces of chicken such as neck, feet, wings and back, used in making chicken stock.

GELATINE: It is obtained from bones of animals or fish, mostly used in jellies and mousses, souffles and creams.

GLAZE: Cover foods with aspic or with jam or sugar syrup.

JULIENNE: Meats and vegetables cut in long thin strips as used in Chinese cooking, beef strogonoff and also for garnishing soups.

KIRSH: A cherry liqueur used in flavouring fruits and icecreams, particularly pineapple.

MACEDOINE: Mixture of vegetables or fruits.

MARINATE: To soak in mixture of oil, vinegar, seasonings, used for raw meats and fish, also fruits soaked in syrup.

MARZIPAN: Confections of almonds and sugar.

[preceding line, top of right column:] with a sieve, or dredge flour whilst rolling the dough.

MIRPOIX: — Cooking gently in butter or any other fat for a few minutes.

MOUSSE: — Mixture of meats, vegetables or fruits, made with cream and gelatine.

PUREE: — Any meats, fish, vegetables or fruits blended to a creamy consistency.

POUSSIN: — Spring chicken.

PANADA: — Paste of flour and water, for thickening soups.

PATE DE FOIGRAS: — Paste made from goose liver.

PAYSANNE: — Farm style dish.

PETIT FOURS: — Small iced cakes or cookies, served after dinner with ice-cream or dessert.

PIMENTO: — Red peppers used for relish and for flavouring dishes.

POACH: — To cook in hot liquid, under boiling point, the liquid must cover the food, mostly used for fish.

ROUX: — A mixture of flour and butter, used in thickening gravies.

RAGOUT: — A thick french stew.

RAMEKINS: — Small individual baking dishes.

RENNET: — Used for curdling or coagulating milk.

SKIM: — To remove scum or fat from the surface of stocks, soups and jam.

STOCK: — Made from meats, fish, vegetables with water, simmered for a few hours, strained and used for soups and gravies.

SAUTE: — To cook in very little fat.

SCALDING: — Putting briefly into boiling water, more so fruits which have to be peeled (like apricots and peaches).

SHORTENING: Margarine or any solidified
                       oil used in making cakes, bis-
                       cuits and pastries.

TRUSS: To skewer the legs and wings
                       of poultry, or tie it with a
                       string, easier for cooking and
                       serving.

APPROXIMATE WEIGHTS AND MEASURES

STANDARD MEASURING CUP AND SPOONS:			ALL MEASUREMENTS ARE LEVEL UNLESS OTHER-WISE STATED:
One 8 oz. cup	=	½ pint	

1 tsp	=	5 gms			
1 tbsp	=	15 „			
2 tbsp	=	30 „			
4 tbsp	=	¼ cup		=	50 gms.
8 tbsp	=	½ „		=	100 „
16 tbsp	=	1 „		=	200 „
1 lb	=	16 oz.		=	455 „
1 kilo	=	2 lb.	2 oz.	=	1000 „
			1 oz.	=	30 „

LIQUID MEASUREMENTS

1 cup	=	½ pint		=	¼ lit
2 cups	=	1 „		=	½ „
4 cups	=	2 pints		=	1 „

TABLE OF EQUIVALENTS

Butter 2 cups	=	1 lb.		=	455 gms.
„ 1 cup	=	½ lb.		=	227 „
„ ½ „	=	¼ lb.		=	115 „
Breadcrumbs 8 cups	=	1 lb.		=	455 „
Brown sugar, firmly packed 2-¼ cups	=	1 lb.		=	455 „
Castor sugar 3-½ cup	=	1 lb.		=	455 „
Icing sugar 4 cups	=	1 lb.		=	455 „
Cheese dry 4 cups	=	1 lb.		=	455 „
Cheese fresh 5 cups	=	1 lb.		=	455 „
Cocoa 4 cups	=	1 lb.		=	455 „
Chocolate grated 5 tbsp.	=	1 oz.		=	30 „
Cottage cheese 2 cups	=	1 lb.		=	455 „
Dates pitted 2 cups	=	1 lb.		=	455 „
Eggs large 5 whole	=	1 cup			

Eggs whites 8	=	1 cup		
Eggs yolks 16	=	1 cup		
Flour 4 cups	=	1 lb.	=	455 gms
Granulated sugar 2 cups	=	1 lb.	=	455 „
Lemon juice 1 lemon	=	2 tbsp.		
Pinch of salt ⅛ tsp.				
Raisins seedless 3 cups	=	1 lb.	=	455 „
Rice 2-¼ cups	=	1 lb.		
Walnuts chopped 3 cups	=	1 lb.	=	455 „

ABBREVIATIONS

tsp	=	teaspoon
dsp	=	desertspoon
tbsp	=	tablespoon

OVEN TEMPERATURE

		Fahrenheit	Centigrade	Gas
Very hot	=	475 - 450	250	8 - 9
Hot	=	450 - 375	200	6 - 7
Moderate	=	375 - 300	175	3, 4, 5
			150	
Slow	=	300 - 250	125	1, 2
Very slow	=	250 - 200	100	½

GLOSSARY OF HINDI TERMS

English	Hindi
Alum	Fadki
Almonds	Badam
Apples	Safarjan
Apricots	Zardaloo
Asofoetida	Hing
Allspice	Kebab chini
Barley	Jowari
Bayleaf	Tejpatta
Beef	Gai ka gosht
Beans	Sena
Beetroot	Chukunda
Black pepper	Kala mirchi
Black lentil	Kala masoor
Bones	Haddi
Brain	Bheja
Brinjal	Baingan
Brown sugar	Lal sakar
Butter	Muska
Butter milk	Chas
Basil	Tulsi leaves
Candy sugar	Khari sakar
Cardamom	Elaichi
Carroway seeds	Shahjeera
Cauliflower	Phoolgobie
Cayenne Pepper	Lal mirchi powder
Celery	Kurufus
Chicken	Moorgi
Chilis	Mirchi
Charoli	Chorongi
Chutney	Chutney
Cinnamon	Taj or Dalchini
Clarified butter	Ghee
Cloves	Lavang

GLOSSARY OF HINDI TERMS

English	Hindi
English	*Hindi*
Coconut	Nariel or Khopra
Coriander	Dhanya
Coriander leaves	Kothmir
Corn	Makai bootha
Cream of wheat	Sooji
Cucumber	Kheere
Curd	Dahi
Cream	Malai
Cummin seed	Jeera
Cashew nuts	Kajoo
Caper	Kardo
Cochineal	Khirmaj
Cottage cheese	Paneer
Dates	Khajoor
Dough	Gundha atta
Duck	Badak
Dried haricot beans	Lobia
Drumstick	Sekta-ni-sing
Essence	Khushboo
Fat	Churbee
Fennel	Variali
Fenugreek	Methee
Figs	Anjeer
Fish	Machi
Flour	Maida
Fowl	Murgi
French beans	Falli
Fishroe	Garab
Fine vermicelli	Sev
Garlic	Lason
Ginger	Adrak
Ginger powder	Soonth
Gram	Channa
Grapes	Angoor
Green chillies	Hara mirchi
Green peas	Vatana

English	Hindi
Gram flour	Besan
Gravy	Ras
Herbs	Masala sookka patta ka
Horse radish	Mooli safed
Ham	Suvar ka gosht
Ice	Baraf
Jaggery	Goor
Kidneys	Goorda
King prawns	Sondhia
Lamb	Bakra
Lemon	Bara nimboo
Lentil red	Masoor dahl
Lentil yellow	Tuvar Dahl
Lettuce	Salad-Kalu
Liver	Kaleja
Lobster	Sahn or Bara Jinga
Leaves Arvi	Aloo ka patta
Mango	Aam
Meat	Gosht
Mint	Pudina
Mullet	Boi
Mustard	Rai
Mustard seeds	Sarso
Mushrooms	Goochi
Milk	Doodh
Mace	Javantri
Mackerel	Bhangra
Nutmeg	Jaiphul
Onion	Pyaz
Orange	Narangi or Santra
Parsley	Ajmood
Pear	Nashpati

English	*Hindi*
Peach	Aroo
Peanuts	Mungfali
Pickle	Achar
Pineapple	Annanas
Plums	Aloo bokhara
Pistachio	Pista
Pomfret fish	Chamna
Poppy seed	Khuskhus
Potato	Aloo or Batata
Prawns	Jinga
Puffed rice	Kurmurra
Pumpkin	Kadoo
Radish	Mooli
Raisin	Kismis
Rosewater	Gulab ka pani
Saffron	Zaffran or Kesar
Sago	Saboo dana
Saltpetre	Shore
Sesame	Till
Sour lime	Nimboo
Spinach	Bhaji
Sweet potato	Sakarkan
Tamarind	Imli
Thyme	Ajmo
Tongue	Jaban
Turmeric	Haldi
Vinegar	Seerka
Walnuts	Akhrot
White of an egg	Safedi
Whey	Chas
Yeast	Khameer
Yolk of an egg	Zardee
Yellow colouring	Jelebi ka rang

HORS D'OEUVRES

Hors d'oeuvres are appetisers, served before a meal with drinks.

They can also be served as a first course to a sit down dinner.

If served with drinks they should be prepared in little bits that can be served on toothpicks, or easily handled with the fingers.

If they are to be served hot, keep them hot in the oven and serve few at a time.

If they are to be served cold, chill them well.

Do not serve too many as it will dull the appetite for a good dinner; they are really meant to whet your appetite and make you look forward to a good meal.

SHRIMPS ON TOAST

2 cups small shrimps
4 slices lean bacon
6 water chestnuts
¼ tsp mono sodium
    glutamet
12 slices bread trimmed
    of crust

1 egg
1 tbsp cornflour
1 tsp soya sauce
1 tbsp brandy or sherry
¼ tsp pepper
Oil for frying

Mince bacon and shrimps together into a paste, add brandy, S. sauce, pepper, M. glutamet, cornflour, finely chopped chestnuts and egg (If liked, add 1 green chopped chilli).

Apply the above paste equally on 12 slices of bread. Heat oil, then fry the slice's paste downwards first on a slow fire, turn the slices and fry the other side. Remove and drain on absorbent paper.

Serve hot, cut into slices or squares (to be served on picks).

Will serve ten to twelve people.

PICKLED OYSTERS

3 dozen oysters
1 capsicum sliced
12 peppercorns
2 cups cider vinegar

1 doz tiny white onions
2 tsp. salt
3 bay leaves

Shell and clean the oysters, place them in a bowl and pour boiling water over them to cover, leave for 2 minutes, then drain well.

Put vinegar, peppercorns, salt and bay leaves in a saucepan, give it one boil and cool.

Take a jar with a fitting lid, place the oysters in it, pour over it the cooled vinegar, add to it peeled onions and sliced capsicum.

Place in the refrigerator for 3 days. Serve cold on picks.

Will serve six people.

FISH APPETIZER IN RUM

*1 kilo piece of ghol or
any other firm white
fish
2 tsp salt*

*1 cup water
Juice of 4 lemons
¼ cup rum
1 dsp salt*

Cut fish into small cubes, wash, add salt to the water
and soak the pieces of fish in it for 2 hours, then drain
the fish and rinse in fresh water, place in a bowl and
cover with lemon juice and rum.

Keep overnight in the refrigerator.

Serve, sprinkled with freshly ground pepper.

Will serve eight to ten people.

RAW FISH APPETIZER

*½ kilo piece of ghol fish
½ cup olive oil
3 green chillies finely
chopped
3 tbsp. coriander finely
chopped
6 slices garlic finely
chopped*

*½ cup finely sliced spring
onions
½ tsp freshly ground
pepper
½ cup lemon juice
1 tsp salt
½ tsp tobasco*

Cut fish into julienne strips, put in a glass dish, add
lemon juice and leave it in the refrigerator overnight,
turning once or twice in the day. Next day drain off
the liquid, then add all the above ingredients and toss
well. Chill and sprinkle with some fresh coriander leaves
before serving.

This makes a very nice party dish, but do not tell your
guests that it is raw fish. After they eat, you may men-
tion it. All my guests so far have enjoyed it.

Will serve eight to ten people.

TOMATO COCKTAIL

*2 kilos red ripe tomatoes
¼ cup chopped spring
onions
1 dsp salt
2 tbsp. sugar*

*½ cup chopped celery
1 large capsicum chop-
ped
2 tbsp W. sauce*

Chop tomatoes, add to them the celery, onions and capsicum; add 3 cups water and salt and bring to a boil and then let it simmer for an hour.

Cool a little and blend in a blender, strain through a fine sieve. Add W. sauce, sugar, and boil for 5 minutes. Chill and serve.

Will serve twelve to fourteen people.

GRAPE COCKTAIL

2 cups seedless grapes	1 cup cottage cheese
¼ cup cream	1 tbsp sugar
1 dsp rum	pinch of salt

Wash grapes and dry them.

Beat cheese, cream, salt and sugar, add rum.

Divide grapes into six cocktail glasses, cover with the cheese mixture, sprinkle some brown sugar over it. Chill and serve.

This makes a good first course.

Will serve eight people.

PRAWN COCKTAIL

2 cups boiled prawns	½ cup tomato ketchup,
1 tbsp lemon juice	6 drops tobasco
1 tbsp grated spring onions	2 tbsp finely chopped celery
2 tsp W. sauce	½ tsp salt

Mix all the above ingredients, chill and serve in individual glasses. Sprinkle with some chopped parsley.

Will serve eight people.

LOBSTER COCKTAIL

2 cups boiled chopped lobsters	salt
	¾ cup mayonnaise
½ cup cream	3 tbsp tomato ketchup
1 tsp tobasco	1 dsp W. sauce
1 tsp chilli sauce	1 tbsp lemon juice

Mix all the above ingredients, chill and serve in individual glasses over a bed of finely shredded lettuce. Sprinkle with some very finely chopped spring onions.
Will serve eight people.

OYSTER COCKTAIL—I

2 cups fresh cleaned oysters	a few drops tobasco
3 tbsp lemon juice	½ cup tomato ketchup
2 tbsp chopped green onions	3 tbsp. salad oil
2 tbsp chopped parsley	1 tbsp chopped chives
	1 dsp W. sauce
	salt

Mix all the above ingredients except oysters, and chill. Chill oysters separately. Just before serving, divide oysters into six cocktail glasses, and pour sauce over it, sprinkle with chopped parsley.
Will serve six to eight people.

OYSTER COCKTAIL—II

Two cups chilled oysters, ¾ cup sherry, pinch of salt, pepper. Mix sherry, salt and pepper. Just before serving, pour over chilled oysters.
Will serve six people.

CHEDDAR CHEESE SPREAD

¼ kilo grated cheddar cheese	3 slices garlic
1 tsp dry mustard	1 dsp W. sauce
½ tsp salt	¼ tsp freshly ground pepper
½ cup dry vermouth or beer	

Put all the above ingredients in a blender and blend smooth.

Fill a glass pot with it, smoothen the surface and pour some clarified butter over it to cover the top completely. Keep in the refrigerator for a few weeks, serve as spread.

To clarify butter:

Melt butter over low heat, when it boils, remove from fire and let it settle for a while until clear butter comes to the top. Carefully drain off top butter, leaving the dregs at the bottom. Use as required.

CHEDDAR SHERRY DIP

1 cup cheddar cheese
1 tsp dry mustard
¼ cup sherry
½ cup soft butter

¼ tsp cayenne
1 tsp pepper
salt

Blend all in a blender and serve with chips or salty crackers.
Will serve six to eight people.

EASY CHEESY DIP

¼ kilo cream cheese
1 tbsp finely chopped capsicum
1 tbsp finely chopped spring onion

2 tbsp any chutney, (mango, apple, orange etc.)
2 tbsp tomato ketchup
2 dsp W. sauce.

Mix all the above ingredients and serve in a bowl with either potato chips or any salty biscuits.
It can also be served, spread on biscuits, garnished with an olive or pickled onion.
Will serve six to eight people.

CHEESY CHICKEN LIVER SPREAD

¼ kilo chicken liver
2 tbsp grated cheese
¼ tsp pepper

2 tbsp butter
¼ tsp salt
2 tbsp rum

Clean and wash chicken livers and saute in melted butter until it is browned and cooked; do this on slow fire, when cooked. Cool and blend in a blender with cheese, salt, pepper and rum. Serve on biscuits.

CURRIED CHEESE DIP

1 cup cottage cheese
1 tsp curry powder
2 tbsp chopped mango
  chutney
1 tbsp brandy or rum

1 cup processed cheese
2 tbsp finely chopped
  spring onion
salt
¼ tsp pepper

Blend all in a blender and serve with potato chips or crackers.

Will serve eight to ten people.

CHEESE DIP FOR COCKTAIL SAUSAGES

¼ kilo cheddar cheese
1 tbsp flour
1 tsp mustard powder
2 tbsp chopped onion
½ kilo cocktail sausages
  or frankfurters cut into
  small pieces
2 tbsp butter

¼ tsp salt and pepper
  each
2 egg yolks
½ cup beer or milk (a
  little more may be
  needed to get the right
  consistency)

Combine grated cheese, salt, pepper, mustard and flour. Melt butter in a saucepan, take it off fire, then add all the mixed ingredients, mix well, then add milk or beer gradually, do not make it lumpy, then put it over low heat and cook, stirring constantly, until thick; then take it off fire and beat in egg yolks.

Just before serving, heat it over low heat, if lumpy, strain.

Serve as dip for the sausages which have been warmed up, not fried. To warm sausages, put them in a pan and just give it a boil or warm them in a slow oven with a little water.

Canned sausages can be used; boil the can in hot water.

Will serve ten to twelve people.

SALAMI SAUSAGE ROLLS

½ cup cream cheese
1 tbsp finely chopped
  spring onion
¼ kilo thinly sliced
  salami

¼ cup thick cream
1 tbsp finely chopped
  capsicum
¼ tsp salt and pepper
  each

Make the filling by blending cream cheese, cream, onion, capsicum, salt and pepper. Put this mixture on each slice of salami and roll, pierce a pick and chill. Serve for cocktails or as hors-d'oeuvre.
Will serve eight to ten people.

SPAM OR SALAMI ROLLS

½ tin spam or ¼ kilo
  salami
2 tbsp cream
1 tbsp chopped spring
  onion

1 dsp chopped gherkins
¼ kilo cream cheese
1 tsp W. sauce
salt, pepper, pinch chilli
  powder

Mix cream cheese with all the seasonings and beat well, chill.
Slice spam or salami into thin slices, shape each slice into a cornucopia, fill with cheese mixture and put a pick to hold shape. Chill well; before serving, remove the picks and put an olive or half a walnut in the centre.
Will serve eight to ten people.

ROLL MOPS

6 mackerel fish
12 small gherkins
1 small onion cut into
  four
1 piece cinnamon
¼ cup salt
4 slices garlic

1 cup white vinegar
1 red chilli
6 peppercorns
4 cloves
1 cup water
4 bay leaves

Make 12 fillets from the mackerels and wash them well.

Mix salt with water, soak the fillets in this brine for an hour, then drain well and wipe with clean cloth. Place a gherkin on each fillet and roll up, skin side up; pierce a pick in each roll, place them in a glass bowl. Boil vinegar with all spices for about 10 min., cool and pour over the roll mops. Cover the dish with foil.

Keep them in the refrigerator, turn them in the liquid at least once a day. Serve after 4 days.

Fittingly served as a first course, or as hors-d'oeuvre. *Will serve six people.*

OYSTER SURPRISE

6 *small sized oranges or lemons*	3 *doz oysters*
2 *tbsp chopped spring onion*	3 *tbsp lemon juice*
	½ *cup thick cream*
1 *tsp freshly ground pepper*	¼ *tsp tobasco*

Cut tops from oranges or lemons, and scoop out all pulp. Place these in a muffin pan.

Poach oysters in their own juice with a tbsp of water for a few minutes or until the edges curl. Remove oysters and strain the juice. To the juice add salt, pepper, lemon juice, onions and cream; mix all this with oysters, spoon the mixture into shells, cover the top with the following sauce and broil the top for a few minutes, or until the top browns a little.

Serve hot immediately.
Will serve six people.

SAUCE

Beat over hot water 3 egg yolks, salt and 1 tbsp lemon juice, add 4 tbsp butter gradually into pieces, remove from hot water, add ½ cup thick cream, and use. Small sweet limes can be used instead of lemons or oranges.

SHRIMPS IN SHERRY—1

2 cups cleaned shrimps
1 tbsp chopped spring
  onion
1 tbsp chopped chives
1 tbsp chopped parsley
2 dsp butter or salad oil

1 tsp chopped garlic
1 tsp mustard powder
½ tsp freshly ground
  pepper
1 dsp salt
½ cup sherry

Melt butter in a pan and dryfry cleaned shrimps until
they become pink, add all the above ingredients except
sherry and parsley, and keep turning over a slow fire,
until all the liquid dries up.

Keep it aside, just before serving heat it, add sherry
and serve hot over slices of lightly fried toast or with
brown bread and butter sandwiches. Sprinkle with
chopped parsley.

Will serve six to eight people.

SHRIMPS IN SHERRY—II

2 cups cleaned shrimps
1 dsp lemon juice
¼ tsp chopped garlic
¼ cup salad oil
¼ tsp salt

¼ cup sherry
2 dsp soya sauce
¼ tsp chopped fresh
  ginger
1 tsp sugar

Mix all the above ingredients and keep for an hour.
Melt 1 tbsp salad oil in a fry pan and fry the shrimp
mixture, adding a little marinade at a time, until all is
used up. Serve hot on toast.

Will serve six to eight people.

MARINATED PRAWNS

2 cups cooked prawns
½ cup olive oil
1 tsp mustard powder
2 tbsp chopped parsley
1 tsp sugar
2 tbsp lemon juice

2 tbsp chopped
  spring onions
¼ tsp mace powder
2 tbsp cider vinegar
½ tsp tobasco,
salt, pepper

Mix all the above ingredients and marinate the prawns in it overnight in the refrigerator. Serve sprinkled with parsley.

Will serve six to eight people.

CHICKEN LIVER PATE

½ kilo chicken liver	1 tsp mustard powder
¼ tsp pepper	½ tsp grated mace
½ tsp grated nutmeg	powder
¼ tsp cinnamon powder	6 spring onions
½ peg Cognac	1 tsp salt
½ cup clarified butter	¼ cup chicken stock, or
½ cup butter	use ½ cube

Clean chicken liver, wash and drain well.

Melt butter in a pan, add chopped onion and saute lightly until soft, add chicken liver and keep turning until liver turns pink, then cook for 5 min., add ½ cup chicken stock, give it one boil, then take it off fire, add all the seasonings, mix well, then blend in a blender, strain through a sieve. Turn into a glass pot, smoothen the top and pour clarified butter over the top. Keep in refrigerator.

Use on biscuits for canapes. Or serve as first course with buttered toasts.

MOULDED CHICKEN LIVER PATE

½ kilo chicken liver	½ cup butter
¼ cup boiling water	1 tbsp gelatine
1 sliced onion	1 tsp salt
½ tsp pepper	½ cup water
½ cup sweet sherry	2 egg yolks

Clean chicken liver, wash and drain well. Melt ¼ cup butter in a pan and saute onion and chicken liver until lightly brown. Add ¼ cup sherry, ½ cup water, salt, pepper, and cook until livers are just tender.

Puree livers in a blender, sieve through a coarse strainer. Pour the mixture in a double boiler, cook over warm

water, add egg yolks and ¼ cup butter. Stir constantly
until thick and smooth. Add gelatine which has been
soaked in ¼ cup hot water. Add the remaining sherry
and blend again until smooth. Pour into a chilled and
wet loaf pan, and chill overnight. Unmould next day
and serve sliced or garnish, as you like.
Will serve ten to twelve people.

MUTTON SPREAD

1 cup boiled mutton	2 tbsp chopped onions
2 hardboiled eggs	¼ cup chopped celery
½ tsp mustard powder	1 tbsp lemon juice
12 stuffed olives or 6	salt, pepper
small gherkins	1 dsp W. sauce
a few drops tobasco	2 drops Angostura
¼ cup mayonnaise	bitters

Run the mutton through a mincer, then add all the
ingredients and mix well, put in a blender in small
quantities and make it into a very fine paste, put it in
a glass dish, smoothen the top and pour clarified butter
over it. Keep in the refrigerator. Use for sandwiches
or on biscuits as canapes.

SOUPS

Soups are excellent in cold climates, but not very practical in our hot climate, but there are many cold soups which can be served and make excellent first courses.

Soups can be a meal in themselves, so do not serve very heavy soups, if the dinner courses are many.

Soups are good if the stock used is well made.

Soup stock can be made in advance and frozen.

Soup stock can be made from odd pieces of meat bones, chicken carcase, feet, neck and giblets. Fish bones and trimmings, shin bone or ox-tails.

Clear stock is made from chicken and white meat. Brown stock from beef, and Bouillon from shin bone.

Vegetable soups can be wholly made either from vegetables, or any meat or fish bones can be added.

Cream soups are thick soups to which either cream or milk has been added.

Chowders are very thick soups made with meats, fish, pork or vegetables, potatoes and corn, milk or cream.

To remove grease from the stock, chill it, and when the grease floats on the top and sets, remove it.

A soup made a day before, stored in the refrigerator, and used next day, tastes much better as it absorbs the flavour well.

A few drops of Angustura bitters enhance the flavour of soups. Sherry makes a good addition to certain soups.

Beef or ox-tail soup tastes better if some dry red table wine is added.

Fish and shell fish soups, also bisque and chowders taste better if a dry white table wine is added.

Wines must be added to the soups just before serving. Do not boil the soups after adding wine.

For colouring soup, use caramel or any of the food colours. A little colour makes the soup more appetising. Use sparingly.

GARNISHES FOR SOUPS

Croutons, noodles, rice, cheese balls, sliced sausages, raw vegetables, parsley, chives, mint, lemon slices, small dumplings, toasted almonds, finely chopped hardboiled egg, sour cream, cream, slivers of ham or tongue.

ACCOMPANIMENTS TO SOUPS

Melba toast, crackers, biscuits, french bread heated in the oven and sliced thickly, garlic bread, buttered toast, cheese pastry rounds, crescents of puff pastry, bread rolls (slices of bread buttered, rolled and crispéd in the oven), grated cheese may be sprinkled before rolling.

If the soup becomes too salty, add to it a raw potato cut into pieces, bring the soup to a boil, then remove the potato.

Soups can be thickened with cornflour, rice, barley, flour or egg.

Salt must be adjusted to taste.

FRANK CHOWDER

6 frankfurters
2 slices garlic
2 carrots
6 cups beef or mutton
  stock
salt, pepper

2 onions
2 medium potatoes
3 stalks celery
4 tbsp butter
1 tbsp W. sauce

Chop onions and garlic and saute in butter until soft but not brown. Cut potatoes, carrots in cubes, cut celery into pieces, cut franks into ¼" slices. Add all this with the salt and pepper and the stock to the onion mixture, cover the pan and simmer until the vegetables are cooked, add W. sauce. Serve hot garnished with chopped parsley.

Serve with garlic bread.

Will serve six to eight people.

CREAM OF CORN CHOWDER

1 pkt or tin cream style
  corn
4 peeled and cubed
  potatoes
1 onion

1 tsp sugar
4 slices bacon
2 cups milk
3 tbsp butter
salt, pepper

Melt butter and saute chopped onion and bacon, then add cubed potatoes and 1 cup water, when the potatoes are tender, add corn, milk, sugar, salt and pepper, simmer for ten minutes and serve very hot, sprinkled with chopped parsley.

Will serve six to eight people.

PRAWN BISQUE

2 cups cleaned prawns
4 tbsp butter
6 bay leaves
¼ cup chopped celery
1 dsp sugar
a few drops tobasco
a few drops red colour
4 cups milk

8 peppercorns
3 cloves
2 tbsp flour
2 dsp W. sauce
a few drops Angustura
   bitters
½ cup cream, sherry

Clean prawns, add 1 cup water and juice of 1 lemon and 1 tsp salt and bring to a boil; when the prawns are pink and round, remove them from the liquid, keep aside; to the liquid add peppercorns, cloves, celery, bay leaves and simmer until celery is cooked; then blend this in a blender and strain; to this add prawns and blend in a blender again until prawns are pureed.

Heat butter in a saucepan, add flour and fry a little; then to this add the pureed prawn liquid and bring to a boil, take it off fire and add to it hot milk, stir well, add the rest of the ingredients and a few drops of red colour to make it slightly pink.

Before serving, heat the soup over slow fire while stirring, do not boil. Add cream and sherry after taking off the fire and serve sprinkled with grated nutmeg.

If the mixture curdles, blend again until smooth.

Will serve eight to ten people.

PLUM SOUP (COLD)

1 kilo red ripe plums
8 cups chicken stock
1 piece cinnamon
1½ tsp salt
2 tbsp fine tapioca

¼ cup sugar
4 cloves
½ tsp grated nutmeg
1 lemon thinly sliced
¼ cup sherry or rum

Wash the plums, put in a pan with 6 cups of stock, sugar, cloves, cinnamon, nutmeg, salt and lemon slices; simmer until plums are tender. Remove from fire, cool a little and then remove all the seeds, lemon slices, cin-

namon and cloves. Then blend in a blender, strain. If
sour, add a little more sugar.

Boil the remaining stock, whilst boiling sprinkle tapioca
over it and stir until the mixture is clear. Add to it the
plum mixture, and taste for seasonings. Chill, serve in
individual bowls sprinkled with toasted slivered almonds.
Will serve eight to ten people.

TOMATO VICHYOISE

2 kilos tomatoes	parsley
¼ kilo white onions	½ kilo potatoes
3 slices garlic	4 tbsp butter
1 dsp sugar	4 cups chicken stock
1 dsp salt	1 cup cream
¼ tsp pepper	1 tbsp W. sauce

Peel and cut into cubes potatoes and onions; chop
garlic. Melt butter and saute all this on a slow fire,
stirring occasionally for about 15 min. Wash tomatoes
and chop, add to the above mixture with the stock, salt,
and pepper; simmer for about an hour until tomatoes
and potatoes are soft, then blend in a blender and strain.
Taste seasonings add W. sauce and sugar, then chill.
Before serving, mix with cream.

Serve very cold with chopped parsley.

For vegetarians, omit stock, add water in the same
proportion.

Add a few drops of red colour.
Will serve eight to ten people.

LENTIL SOUP

2 cups split lentils	½ tsp pepper
(masoor dal)	6 bay leaves
1 ham bone or beef shank	2 carrots
or mutton bone	4 cloves
2 onions	1 dsp salt
6 slices garlic	½ cup chopped parsley
2 stalk celery	¼ cup sour cream
6 peppercorns	8 frankfurters
½ cup chopped spring	
onions	

Soap lentils overnight in cold water. Next day wash
and drain lentils, put them in a large pan with the bone,
peeled onions stuck with cloves, salt, bay leaves, peppercorns, garlic, celery and whole carrots. Pour 4 cups
water and simmer over slow fire for about 1½ hours, until
lentils are soft. Remove from fire. Remove bone from
it, if there is any meat on the bone, remove and keep.

Remove from the soup, the onions, celery, bay leaves,
peppercorns and carrot and discard all.

Cut frankfurters in slices and add to the soup, cook
for 10 min. Serve hot, garnished with chopped spring
onions, parsley and a dollop of cream.

The above soup can also be made with whole black
lentils (masoor).

Served with garlic bread, this soup is a meal in itself,
so the other course must be light.

Will serve eight to ten people.

BABY ONION SOUP

1 kilo small white onions
4 tbsp tomato puree
1 cup macaroni pieces
4 dsp butter
¼ kilo bacon

6 cups of any stock
(chicken, mutton, beef
or vegetable)
salt, pepper, parmesan
cheese

Clean the onions and soak in fresh water. Chop bacon
finely, melt butter in a pan, add bacon and the drained
onions and fry until golden. Mix tomato puree with
the stock add this to the onion mixture along with the
macaroni pieces, give it a boil and then simmer over
slow fire until the macaroni is cooked. Season well.
Serve very hot, sprinkled with grated cheese (or any
other cheese may be used).

Stock can be made from the cubes. For a vegetarian
soup, do not use bacon, but use veg. stock.

Will serve six to eight people.

LETTUCE SOUP (COLD)

2 fresh cabbage lettuce
6 sprigs parsley
4 spring onions with
   some green portion
salt, pepper

½ cup good french dress-
   ing
1 bunch watercress
2 cloves garlic
3 cups chicken stock

Marinate lettuce leaves in the french dressing for about 10 min. Chop parsley, watercress, onions and garlic; add all this to the cold chicken stock, then add the marinated lettuce to it and put all in the blender, strain and serve well, chilled with a slice of tomato floating, and a blob of cream over it. Add a few drops of green food colour.

Will serve six to eight people.

PUMPKIN SOUP

1 kilo red pumpkin
6 spring onions minced
1 cup thin cream
a few mint leaves
¼ cup cream for garnish

6 cups chicken stock
2 tsp sugar
salt, pepper
1 tomato
dash Angustura bitters

Cut pumpkin in little cubes, add 1 cup water, cover and cook until soft, drain the water if any remaining. Add the pumpkin to the chicken stock with onions, salt and pepper to taste. Cook all this for 10 min. then blend in a blender and strain. Cool completely, then add 1 cup cream and bitters. Chill, then pour into individual soup bowls.

Just before serving, lay a slice of tomato over it, put two mint leaves over it and pipe a star of cream in the centre. Serve cold.

Will serve eight to ten people.

CHILLED AVOCADO SOUP

6 Avocados	3 cups chicken stock
1 cup cream	2 dsp sugar
1 dsp W. sauce	juice of two lemons
2 dsp flour	2 dsp butter
salt, pepper	

Melt butter add flour, fry a little and add hot chicken stock, stirring continuously, give it one or two boils, remove from fire, cool a little and add peeled and chopped Avocados. Put in a blender and blend until smooth, strain, add cream and seasonings and chill well before serving. Top with some chopped chives.

Taste the avocados before using them, as some of them tend to be bitter. Do not use over-ripe avocados.

Will serve six to eight people.

TOMATO SOUP

1 kilo ripe red tomatoes	a few drops Angostura
2 stalks celery	bitters
1 small onion	1 potato (small)
1 tbsp butter	3 cups water
1 tbsp W. Sauce	1 tbsp flour
¼ tsp freshly ground	2 tbsp sugar
pepper	½ dsp salt
1 large carrot	

Wash tomatoes and cut them into small pieces, scrape the carrot and slice, wash the potato and cut into cubes with the skin, chop celery and onion.

Put all this in a saucepan with salt and water, and give it a boil. Then let it simmer over slow fire for about an hour; while hot, strain it, squeezing out all the juice.

Melt butter, add flour, brown a little, then add the strained juice, give it a boil, stirring it constantly. Add all the seasonings. Strain again through a fine strainer. Heat and serve in soup bowl garnished with a blob of cream or fried bread croutons. Add a little cochineal for colour.

Will serve four to six people.

COLD TOMATO SOUP

2 kilos ripe red tomatoes
½ cup chopped carrots
2 sprigs parsley
4 cloves
1 blade of mace
a few drops tobasco
2 dsp sugar
1 tbsp gelatine to be soaked in a little cold water

1 cup chopped celery
½ cup chopped onions
12 peppercorns
1 small piece cinnamon
1 dsp salt
a few drops Angostura bitters
2 dsp W. sauce
1 egg white

Wash and chop tomatoes, put in a large pan along with celery, carrots, onions, parsley, peppercorns, cinnamon, cloves, mace and salt. Give it a boil, then simmer for an hour or until everything is well cooked. Stir occasionally. Strain through a collander, put it back on the pan, add egg white with the egg shell and give it a boil; then when it clears, strain through a muslin cloth, do not squeeze, let it drip clear, then add sugar gelatine, and give it a boil until gelatine melts. Add the rest of the seasonings. Stir until it cools. Add sherry or brandy for flavour, if desired.

Chill in the refrigerator, serve very cold, sprinkle a few chopped chives.

Add a little cochineal for colour when the soup is cool. Will serve six to eight people.

COLD CHICKEN TOMATO SOUP

2 kilos ripe red tomatoes
2 cups chicken stock
salt, pepper
2 dsp sugar
1 cup cream

6 spring onions
2 tbsp tomato puree
2 cups water
2 dsp flour

Cut tomatoes into pieces, chop onions, put in a pan with water and cook until tomatoes are soft. Strain through a collander. Mix tomato puree with flour to this add the tomato juice and cook for a few minutes; then add chicken stock, salt, pepper and sugar; bring to a boil, then cool, and blend in a blender, strain through a fine sieve, chill; add cream before serving; a little sherry may be added, or it may be served sprinkled with chopped dill leaves, strips of tomatoes.

Add a little cochineal for colour.

Will serve eight to ten people.

SALADS

Lettuce must be fresh and crisp and must be soaked in water with a pinch of permanganate of potash for about ten minutes and then washed under running water. It should then be shaken thoroughly in a collander, the water allowed to drain completely, and the lettuce then rolled in a clean towel and placed in the refrigerator until required. It should be cold and dry before the dressing is poured over it.

Lettuce should never be cut with a knife, but should always be torn into pieces.

Salt, pepper and the dressing must be added just before serving, otherwise the lettuce will wilt. This also helps in retaining its flavour and vitamin content.

Lettuce is best served in a wooden bowl, and must be tossed well after the dressing is added, so that each leaf is coated with it. This may be done gently with a salad spoon and fork.

French dressing is the commonest of all for lettuce leaves. Mayonnaise can also be used instead of french dressing.

Other variations that can be added to the lettuce bowl are sliced radishes, tomatoes, spring onions, celery, hardboiled eggs, carrots, pickled gherkins, cucumber, cheese and beetroot.

Tomatoes and beetroots must be added at the last minute or used just as a garnish.

For making moulded salads, always chill the mould and brush very lightly with salad oil. This facilitates easy removal of the salad from the mould. If the salad is stuck to the mould, it should be inverted on a platter, and a hot towel placed over it until the salad is released.

Moulded salads are very decorative and are a must on a buffet table. They are also very cooling in the hot weather and can be made easily with any leftovers by adding a colourful jelly, or with fresh fruits with some fruit juice and gelatine.

Salads may be garnished with any of the following:

Lettuce leaves, sliced tomatoes, sliced beetroots, cucumbers, parsley, sliced hardboiled eggs, celery, sliced lemons or oranges, stuffed olives, pickled onions, gherkins, cherry tomatoes, spring onions, carrot curls of jullien strips.

JELLIED APPLE SALAD

1 packet lemon jelly
1 tbsp lemon juice
¼ cup chopped celery
1½ cups hot water

2 large red skinned
  apples
¼ cup chopped walnuts

Melt jelly in hot water, add a pinch of salt. Cut apples with the skin in cubes, add them to the jelly with celery and walnuts, mix well, then pour into a wet mould and chill until set.

Unmould on lettuce leaves and serve with orange dressing.

Orange Dressing:

½ cup orange juice, 1 tsp finely chopped orange rind, 1 cup mayonnaise, ½ cup cottage cheese, pinch of salt. Blend all together and chill.

Will serve six to eight people.

MOULDED BEETROOT SALAD

1 packet lemon jelly
1 tbsp sugar
1 tbsp lemon juice
salt, pepper

2 cups cooked beets
  (cut into cubes or
  slices)
½ tsp cinnamon powder

Melt jelly in 1½ cups of hot water; add sugar, lemon juice .cinnamon and seasonings; cool, then add beetroot. Pour into a wet mould and chill until set. Unmould on a platter, surround with shredded lettuce and some carrot curls.

Taste beets before using; if not sweet, add a little more sugar; vinegar can be used instead of lemon juice. A little rum may be added, if liked.

Will serve six to eight people.

WALDORF JELLY SALAD

2 large red skinned apples	½ tsp salt
1½ cups hot water	1 packet orange jelly
1 tbsp sugar	1 tbsp lemon juice
½ cup chopped capsicum	½ cup chopped celery
	¼ cup chopped walnuts

Cut apples into cubes with the skin.

Melt jelly in hot water, add lemon juice and sugar. Cool, stir in all other ingredients with salt, mix well and pour into a wet mould. Chill until set. Serve with Orange Mayonnaise.

Orange Mayonnaise: 1 cup mayonnaise, ½ cup orange juice, ½ cup cream, 1 tsp lemon juice, ¼ tsp salt, a few drops orange food colour.

Mix all and blend, chill and serve. Any orange-flavoured liqueur can be added.

Will serve six to eight people.

PEACH SALAD MOULDED

1 tin sliced peaches	1 packet orange jelly
1 dsp sugar	6 cloves
1 piece cinnamon	2 tbsp vinegar
2 tbsp chopped walnuts	1 tbsp brandy

Drain peaches from syrup, add water to the syrup to make two cups liquid; add to it sugar, cloves and cinnamon and boil for 5 min; add jelly and stir until it dissolves; add vinegar and strain. Cool and chill until partially set. Fold in peaches and walnuts, pour into a wet mould and set. Unmould on a platter and garnish with lettuce leaves.

Serve with mayonnaise.

Will serve six to eight people.

COTTAGE CHEESE RING

1 cup cottage cheese	1 tbsp gelatine
½ cup water	1 cup mayonnaise
½ cup chopped celery	½ cup chopped capsicum
1 tsp sugar	salt, pepper

Melt gelatine in ½ cup water, blend in mayonnaise, cottage cheese, and seasonings. Chill until partially set, fold in celery and capsicum, pour into a chilled mould (ring) and chill.

Unmould on a platter and surround with shredded lettuce and garnish with tomatoes.

Will serve six to eight people.

FRUIT AND COTTAGE CHEESE LOAF

1 cup cottage cheese	½ cup cold water
2 tbsp gelatine	1 tbsp finely chopped
1 tin mixed fruit salad	capsicum
1 tbsp chopped walnuts	¼ tsp salt and pepper
1 tbsp lemon juice	each
1 cup mayonnaise	

Soak gelatine in water, and melt over hot water.

Blend cottage cheese, mayonnaise, salt, pepper, and sugar in a blender, add gelatine, pour into a bowl and fold in fruits, capsicum and walnuts. Pour in a wet loaf pan and set. Unmould and garnish with lettuce.

Drain fruit from syrup and use ½ cup syrup instead of water to soak gelatine.

Fresh fruit can be used.

Will serve eight to ten people.

PEAR CHERRY AND CIDER SALAD

1 tin pears	1 tin cherries
1 pint apple cider	2 tbsp sugar
2 tbsp lemon juice	2 tbsp rum
pinch of salt	

Drain pears and soak them in apple cider for an hour, then drain them thoroughly, keeping aside cider.

Drain cherries and put them, keep the juice.

Mix pear and cherry juice and measure it, take 1 dsp of gelatine to a cup of juice.

Soak gelatine in ½ cup cold water, to this add pear and cherry juice, sugar, salt and lemon juice, stir over hot water until gelatine is melted. Cool the liquid and then add rum.

Arrange some pears and cherries in the bottom of a wet mould, pour a little gelatine mixture over it and let it set, so that the fruit will stay in place.

To the remaining gelatine mixture, add chopped pears, pitted cherries. Pour over the set mixture. Chill until set.

Unmould and garnish with some lettuce.

Serve with mayonnaise.

Will serve eight to ten people.

ORANGE CREAM MOULD

1 pkt orange jelly	1 cup hot water
1 cup cream cheese	½ cup orange juice
1 dsp finely grated	1 tbsp lemon juice
orange rind	8 slices pineapple

Dissolve jelly in hot water, add lemon juice, ¼ tsp salt and 1 tbsp castor sugar; when cool mix in cream cheese, orange juice and rind and blend well, pour into 8 small moulds and chill.

Drain pineapple slices, arrange on a platter and unmould each orange mould on the pineapple slices and garnish with lettuce leaves; if liked, a little cream may be piped around the edge of the moulds over the pineapple.

A little orange liqueur may be added to the cheese mixture.

Will serve eight people.

ORANGE CREAM SALAD

1 pkt orange jelly
1 cup orange juice
1 cup cottage cheese
1 tbsp sugar
1 dsp Cointrau or any
orange liqueur

1 cup hot water
1 tsp finely grated orange
rind
½ cup mayonnaise
pinch of salt

Dissolve jelly in hot water add orange juice and sugar, let it cool, then add cottage cheese, rind and mayonnaise, blend all smooth. Pour into a wet mould and chill overnight.

Unmould and decorate with sliced oranges.

It can be set in a glass dish and the top decorated with cream and orange sections.

Will serve six to eight people.

FRUIT SALAD IN CREAM CHEESE

1 cup melon balls
1 cup pineapple pieces
1 cup cottage cheese
1 dsp sugar

1 cup seedless grapes
½ cup sliced bananas
½ cup mayonnaise
pinch of salt, pepper

Combine melon, grapes and pineapple and chill.

Mix cheese, mayonnaise with salt, pepper and sugar and blend smooth. Just before serving, mix the fruits with the cheese mixture; lastly, slice bananas and add. Serve in a melon shell. Garnish the top with some cherries and mint leaves.

Do not add bananas much before it is served as it will turn black.

Will serve eight to ten people.

CURRIED RICE SALAD

2 cups cooked rice
1 cup chopped celery
½ cup chopped spring
onions
1 dsp curry powder
1 tbsp lemon juice

salt, pepper
2 cups cooked prawns
¼ cup chopped capsicum
1 cup french dressing
1 tbsp W. sauce
¼ cup chopped gherkins

Mix all the above ingredients together and chill well. Serve in a glass dish garnished with lettuce leaves and tomato slices.

Instead of capsicum green chillies may be added.

Will serve ten to twelve people.

RICE AND HAM SALAD

2 cups cooked rice
½ cup cooked green peas
½ cup chopped capsicum
¼ cup chopped olives
¼ tsp cayenne pepper
¼ kilo cooked ham

½ cup chopped celery
½ cup finely sliced spring onions
1 cup french dressing
salt, pepper

Cut ham into cubes and mix with all the above ingredients. Chill well; just before serving, add to it a few tender lettuce leaves.

Garnish with hardboiled eggs and stuffed olives.

Will serve ten to twelve people.

FRENCH BEANS SALAD—I

½ kilo french beans
3 hard boiled eggs
4 slices finely chopped bacon

¼ kilo carrots
1 cup sliced spring onions
salt, pepper

Dressing:

¾ cup salad oil
¼ tsp salt
¼ cup vinegar or lemon juice

1 tsp mustard
¼ tsp pepper
2 dsp castor sugar

Blend all this in a blender or shake in a bottle.

String french beans and cut them into halves lengthwise, slice carrots into long strips. Parboil both, and drain well. (Do not overcook). It must stay crisp, cool, add sliced onions, pour dressing over and toss well, chill. Just before serving, add chopped eggs and crisply fried bacon.

Will serve ten to twelve people.

FRENCH BEAN SALAD—II

½ kilo french beans
½ cup pickled onions
½ cup sliced stuffed
  olives

½ cup pure vinegar
½ cup sesame seeds
salt, pepper

Grind sesame seeds in vinegar and keep aside.

String french beans and cut them in pieces, and parboil them. Keep them crisp, cool, add olives, onions, salt and pepper. Then add sesame seed paste and toss well.

Place in a bowl, sprinkle with a few sesame seeds and chopped parsley. Chill and serve.

Will serve six to eight people.

PICKLED BEET SALAD

2 large cooked beets
½ cup brown sugar
¼ tsp clove powder

½ cup vinegar
1 tsp cinnamon powder
salt, pepper

Cut beets into cubes. Combine vinegar, sugar and spices, and bring to a boil, pour over beets and chill. Serve with a few pickled onions on top.

Will serve six to eight people.

BEETROOTS IN MUSTARD SAUCE

Two large beets cooked and cut into slices.

Mustard Sauce:

1 dsp mustard powder
½ cup water
1 dsp flour
1 tbsp butter

1 dsp sugar
¼ cup vinegar
1 egg yolk
½ tsp salt

Mix mustard, flour, sugar, salt with water and vinegar, cook over low heat until thick, then beat in egg yolk and butter, strain and pour over beets.

It can be served either hot or cold.

Will serve six to eight people.

CABBAGE COLE SLAW

4 cups finely shredded
   cabbage
¼ cup vinegar
½ cup finely sliced spring
   onions

½ cup finely sliced celery
½ cup mayonnaise
1 tbsp sugar
salt, pepper

Combine vinegar, mayonnaise, sugar, salt and pepper, and pour over the mixture of cabbage, onion and celery, toss well. Serve on lettuce greens, garnished with capsicum rings, or sliced tomatoes.

Will serve eight to ten people.

CARROT SLAW

1 kilo carrots, scrapped,
   and grated into fine
   strips
½ cup finely minced
   spring onions
1 dsp finely chopped
   green chillies

2 tbsp chopped coriand-
   er leaves
¼ cup vinegar
½ cup salad oil
1 tbsp sugar
salt, pepper

Mix all the above ingredients together and serve over lettuce leaves.

Capsicum and parsley can be used instead of chillies and coriander.

Will serve eight to ten people.

FRUITY CABBAGE SLAW

3 cups shredded cabbage
1 grape fruit or oranges
   peeled and sectioned
½ cup chopped celery
1 tbsp vinegar

salt, pepper
1 cup thinly sliced
   apples
½ cup mayonnaise
1 dsp sugar

Combine cabbage with fruits. Blend mayonnaise, vinegar, sugar, salt and pepper. Pour over veg. and fruit mixture; toss well, serve on lettuce leaves, garnish with olives or tomatoes.

Will serve eight to ten people.

HERBED TOMATOES

6 large red tomatoes
¼ cup vinegar
½ tsp coarsely ground
   pepper

½ cup salad oil
½ tsp salt
¼ tsp mixed herbs
1 tsp sugar

Soak tomatoes in hot water and peel them, then slice thickly.

Mix all the other ingredients in a bowl. Place slices of tomatoes in a serving bowl and pour the dressing over it, chill for 1-2 hours and serve, sprinkled with chopped parsley and a few sliced onions.

Herbs can be omitted.

Will serve six to eight people.

HAM AND EGG SALAD

Ham Salad:

2 cups chicken stock
2 cups chopped ham
2 tbsp chopped gherkin
salt, pepper

2 dsp gelatine
2 tbsp chopped onion
1 tbsp W. sauce

Egg Salad:

8 hard boiled eggs
1 tbsp chopped onion
¼ cup chopped capsicum
¼ cup water
salt, pepper

1 cup mayonnaise
1 tbsp chopped olives
1 tbsp gelatine
¼ cup hot water

Chop eggs finely. Soak gelatine in cold water, then add hot water to melt. Add this to the mayonnaise with all the seasonings, fold in the eggs, onion, capsicum and olives, mix well. Pour all this in a wet loaf pan and chill until set.

Melt gelatine in hot chicken stock, add all the other ingredients and pour over the set egg mixture (cool before pouring over the set mixture). Chill overnight or for a few hours. Unmould and garnish.

Serve mayonnaise separately.

Will serve ten to twelve people.

HAM AND MACARONI SALAD

1 cup chopped ham
1 cup mayonnaise
2 cups boiled macaroni
  pieces

½ cup chopped onion
1 cup chopped parsley
salt, pepper

Toss all the above ingredients together and serve over lettuce leaves. Garnish with sliced tomatoes.
A few stuffed olives may be added.
Will serve eight to ten people.

POTATO AND TONGUE SALAD

2 cups diced cooked
  potatoes
2 cups diced cooked
  tongue
½ cup chopped celery
½ cup sliced gherkins
3 hardboiled eggs

1 cup mayonnaise
1 tsp sugar
2 tsp prepared mustard
salt
6 peppercorns, freshly
  crushed

Chop eggs roughly, combine with potatoes and celery, add gherkins, sprinkle salt, pepper and sugar, toss well. Blend mayonnaise with prepared mustard and add to the potato mixture; add tongue and mix well, chill.
Garnish with carrot curls.
Will serve eight to twelve people.

CHICKEN AND ALMOND SALAD

2 cups diced cooked
  chicken
½ cup chopped celery
½ cup chopped gherkins
1 cup mayonnaise

½ cup toasted almonds
½ cup chopped olives
2 hardboiled eggs sliced
salt, pepper

Combine all the above ingredients except almonds and mayonnaise, season with salt and pepper, toss well, add mayonnaise and mix. Just before serving mix in almonds. Serve over lettuce leaves.
Will serve six to eight people.

CHICKEN SALAD MOULDED

2 cups cooked diced
  chicken
½ cup chopped celery
1 cup mayonnaise
¼ cup water
3 dsp lemon juice
salt, pepper

¼ cup diced capsicum
½ cup sliced stuffed
  olives
2 dsp gelatine
½ cup hot water
1 dsp sugar

Soak gelatine in water, then add hot water and dissolve. Add to the mayonnaise, salt, pepper and sugar, mix well, fold in the other ingredients, pour into a wet mould and chill.

Unmould and garnish with lettuce, tomatoes and olives.
Will serve six to eight people.

PRAWN AND POTATO SALAD

2 cups boiled prawns
½ cup chopped spring
  onions
½ cup chopped celery
2 tbsp chopped parsley
½ cup chopped olives

2 cups boiled cubed
  potatoes
½ cup chopped gherkins
1 cup mayonnaise
salt, pepper

Mix all the above ingredients together and press the mixture in a loose bottom cake pan. Chill, invert on a platter, apply some finely chopped parsley around the sides of the mould. Garnish the top with some sliced hardboiled eggs and a few prawns. Surround the platter with some lettuce, tomatoes and beets.
Will serve eight to ten people.

OYSTER AND RICE SALAD

2 cups cooked rice
½ cup salad oil
1 dsp lemon juice
1 dsp sugar
2 tbsp sliced capsicum
salt, pepper

1 cup cooked oysters
¼ cup vinegar
1 dsp chopped garlic
1 tsp curry powder
2 tbsp spring onion,
  sliced

Mix all the ingredients together, toss well and chill. Serve on lettuce leaves.
Will serve six to eight people.

MUTTON AND APPLE SALAD

2 cups small cubes of mutton
1 cup diced celery
¼ cup sliced spring onions
1 cup mayonnaise

salt, freshly ground pepper
2 cups cubed apples
¼ cup chopped capsicum
1 tbsp chopped mint leaves
2 tbsp lemon juice

Peel and dice apples, sprinkle with lemon juice, then mix with the rest of the ingredients, chill well and serve, garnished with a sprig of mint.
Will serve eight to ten people.

CUCUMBER SALAD

1 cup peeled and chopped cucumber
1 cup boiling water

salt, pepper
1 pkt lemon jelly
1 dsp sugar

Dissolve jelly in 1 cup hot water, add sugar, salt and a pinch of pepper, cool. Blend cucumber in a blender until smooth, mix with jelly, add a few chopped olives and pour into a wet mould and set. Add a little green food colour. Unmould and serve with the dressing.

Cottage Cheese Dressing:

1 cup cottage cheese
1 tbsp lemon juice
1 tbsp sugar

¼ cup cream
salt, pepper

Blend all. Chill and serve.
Will serve six to eight people.

GRAPES AND CUCUMBER SALAD

1 cup seedless grapes
1 tbsp chopped onion
1 tbsp chopped mint
2 cups curds
1 tbsp vinegar
2 tbsp salad oil

1 cup peeled, seeded and
chopped cucumber
½ cup chopped celery
1 tsp salt
¼ tsp freshly ground
pepper

Strain the liquid from the curd, then whip it smooth, add seasonings, vinegar and salad oil. Add grapes, cucumber, onion and celery, mix well and chill for an hour.

If liked, add 1 tbsp sugar and finely chopped green chilli.

It is good served with any meats.
Will serve eight to ten people.

ONION AND CUCUMBER SALAD

4 white onions sliced
1 dsp finely chopped
garlic
1 tbsp lemon juice
salt, pepper

4 cups thinly sliced
cucumber
¾ cup cream
1 tbsp sugar

Combine onions, cucumber and garlic.

Mix cream with lemon juice, salt, pepper and sugar, pour over the onion mixture, chill well, drain the liquid before serving.

Sprinkle some chopped coriander leaves.
Will serve eight to ten people.

CHOPPED TOMATO SALAD

4 large firm tomatoes
¼ cup chopped coriander
leaves
1 dsp W. sauce
1 tbsp lemon juice
1 dsp sugar

½ cup chopped spring
onions
salt, pepper
¾ cup cream
2 tbsp parmesan cheese

Wash, dry and cut tomatoes into cubes, mix with onions.

Mix cream with lemon juice, salt, pepper, W. sauce and sugar. Pour over tomatoes and toss well, chill. Serve, sprinkled with coriander leaves and cheese.

Cheese can be omitted, if desired or any other cheese can be used.

If liked, add one or two chopped green chillies.

Serve with meats.

Will serve six to eight people.

BRINJAL SALAD

1 large brinjal
4 green chillies
2 tbsp lemon juice
1 dsp sugar
2 onions white

½ cup chopped coriander
leaves
2 tbsp salad oil
salt, pepper

Bake brinjal in an oven until tender. Cut into half and scoop out all the pulp, mash the pulp well with a masher, then add finely chopped onions, coriander and all the other ingredients, mix well and chill for a few hours. Serve with toasts.

Will serve six to eight people.

GREEN PEA SALAD

3 cups boiled green peas
1 cup chopped spring
onion
1 tbsp lemon juice

½ cup chopped celery
top
1 cup mayonnaise
salt, pepper

Mix all together and serve over lettuce leaves. Top with sliced stuffed olives, chill well.

Will serve six to eight people.

AVOCADO SALAD

3 large avocados
½ cup sliced stuffed
  olives

1 tin asparagus
Vainagrate dressing

Peel and slice avocados, cut asparagus into pieces.
Mix all with the dressing, toss well and serve.
Will serve six to eight people.

POTATO AND BEET SALAD

Make one recipe pickled beet salad.
Boil 3 large potatoes, peel and cut them into cubes,
sprinkle salt and pepper and toss.
Drain the beets from juice, and add juice to the potatoes, place the potatoes in a glass bowl and surround
them with a ring of drained beets. Sprinkle with finely
chopped parsley and onions. Serve cold with any meats.
If liked, add 2 dsp of W. sauce to the potatoes.
Will serve eight to ten people.

BEET AND HORSE-RADISH SALAD

2 cups cooked sliced
  beets
1 tbsp grated horse-
  radish
3 dsp sugar
½ tsp caraway seeds

1 cup thinly sliced
  spring onion
½ cup vinegar
¼ cup water
salt, pepper

Arrange slices of beets and onions alternately in a
dish, sprinkle horse-radish and caraway seeds in between
layers.
Mix water, vinegar, sugar, salt and pepper, pour over
the beets, cover dish and chill for several hours.
Drain before serving.
Will serve eight to ten people.

FISH

Fish as a food, is most nutritious and diges-tible. One should use more of it in one's daily menu.

Fresh fish, when prepared immediately, has a most delicious flavour.

Frozen fish loses most of its flavour, but can be used for making cutlets, rissoles or for baked dishes.

To find out if the fish is fresh: the eyes must be bright, the gills must be red, the flesh firm and the scales should not come off easily.

Fresh fish has no unpleasant odour.

Fish must not be overcooked, it must be simmered gently until tender, it must never be fast boiled.

To test if the fish is cooked, pierce with a skewer or fork in the thickest part of the fish.

Prawns must be simmered only till they curl and turn pink; overcooking prawns, toughens them.

Frozen fish must be thawed completely before cooking.

Fish once thawed must not be frozen again, but must be used immediately.

PICKLED SALMON

12 slices salmon
4 dsp curry powder
2 tbsp brown sugar
1 tsp prepared mustard
1 tsp pepper and salt
    each
4 large white onions

½ cup salad oil
1 tsp chilli powder
2 cups cider vinegar
1 tsp cummin, roasted
    and pounded
¼ cup W. sauce

Wash the fish and apply some salt and keep for an hour; then wash again and fry lightly in salad oil on both sides. Slice the onion rings.

Combine curry powder, chilli powder, sugar, mustard, cummin, W. sauce, salt, pepper and vinegar, mix all well. In a glass dish, put 4 slices of fish, over it put 1|3 of the sliced onion rings and pour half of the vinegar mixture over it, repeat this all again until all is used up, it will make 3 such layers, sprinkle some chopped bay leaves over each layer or chopped green chillies if preferred hot. Keep in the refrigerator for 3-4 days. Serve cold as appetizer or as first course with sliced tomatoes, beetroot, and cucumber.

Will serve ten to twelve people.

BAKED FISH WITH ALMOND SAUCE

6 trout or 12 fish fillets
4 tbsp butter

¾ cup breadcrumbs

Clean the fish and apply salt and keep for a while, then wash again; roll in breadcrumbs, and keep for ½ hour. Melt butter and fry the fish over very hot fire until brown on both sides. Then put the fish in a moderate oven and bake until cooked, pour sauce over and serve immediately.

Melt butter, add ½ cup shredded almonds and saute until light brown; add pinch of salt and pepper.

Will serve six people.

SALMON STEAKS WITH BACON

6 slices salmon 1" thick	12 slices bacon
3 onions chopped	½ cup breadcrumbs
6 bay leaves	3 tbsp butter
3 tbsp flour	salt, pepper

Butter a glass baking dish, in it lay 6 slices of bacon (trim the rind), sprinkle onions and bay leaves over it, layer with fish slices. Make paste of butter and flour and spread over the fish, sprinkle over with breadcrumbs, over it put another 6 slices of bacon, put it in a moderate oven and bake until the fish is fork-tender. Serve immediately with a lettuce salad.

Will serve six people.

FISH FILLET TARTS

1 baked pastry shell 9"	2 cups flour
½ cup butter	½ tsp salt
1 egg yolk	

Sift flour and salt, rub in butter and egg yolk, bind with a little water in to a dough, wrap in foil and chill for 15 min. Roll the dough between two sheets of greaseproof paper and line a well greased pie dish with the dough, prick it with a fork and crimp the edge, bake until done.

Filling:

8 fillets of pomfrets or sole	2 cups fish stock made from fish bones
1 cup mushrooms sliced	salt and freshly-ground pepper
2 tbsp chopped spring onions	1 fillet cut in two pieces
	16 spears of asparagus
	1 cup butter

Slice mushrooms, fry in 1 tbsp butter and keep aside Butter a baking dish, place the fillets in it, sprinkle with chopped onions and add 1 cup fish stock and poach the fish in the oven until done, drain the fish from stock.

Put a layer of mushrooms in the baked shell, lay the asparagus over it, then over it place the fish fillets. Cover with the following sauce and brown the top in the oven or under a grill. Serve hot.

SAUCE: Drained fish stock plus 1 cup remaining fish stock to be boiled down to 1 cup, 2 dsp flour ; 1 cup milk; 2 egg yolks; salt, pepper.

Melt butter, add flour and fry for a while, add hot milk and stock, bring to a boil; keep stirring, take it off the fire and cool a little, then beat in egg yolk and seasonings. Add 1 dsp of W. sauce, if liked.

Will serve six to eight people.

FISH AND RICE MAYONNAISE

8 fillets of pomfrets
2 cups shelled cooked
* shrimps*
salt, freshly ground pepper

1 cup long grain rice
¼ cup water
juice of 1 lemon
½ cup french dressing

Place fillets in a buttered dish, sprinkle with lemon juice, salt, and pepper, pour water over it and poach in a moderate oven for 20 min. allow to cool in the liquid and drain.

Curry Cream Sauce:

2 cups mayonnaise
1 tbsp tomato ketchup
1 onion, finely chopped
2 tbsp apricot jam
a few sliced olives

¼ cup salad oil
1 tbsp curry powder
6 slices garlic
salt, pepper
slices of lemon

Heat salad oil and fry onion and chopped garlic, add curry powder, seasonings, tomato ketchup and ½ cup water, simmer for 10 min. stir in apricot jam and boil for 1 min. strain and cool. Mix in the mayonnaise.

Boil rice and drain, stir in boiled shrimps, salt, pepper and french dressing, spread rice on a flat serving dish, arrange fish fillets on top of it, and pour curry sauce over it all. Serve cold garnished with olives and lemon slices.

If any sauce remains, serve separately.

Will serve eight to ten people.

FISH CAKES IN MUSHROOM SAUCE

2 cups any cooked white fish	½ tsp cayenne
½ cup mashed potato	1 tbsp W. sauce
1 tsp salt	½ cup breadcrumbs
½ tsp pepper	2 chopped green chillies
	2 eggs

Sauce:

1 cup white sauce	1 cup chopped mush-
a few olives or pimento	rooms

Flake fish and mix with breadcrumbs, chillies, salt, pepper, cayenne and W. sauce, mix and add potato and eggs, beat all well, form into flat cakes, fry in oil.

Fry mushrooms in 1 tbsp butter and add white sauce, salt, and pepper.

Put cakes in a serving dish and pour mushroom sauce over it, garnish with olives or pimento or green capsicum will do.

Will serve eight to ten people.

COLD PRAWN AND RICE MOULD

2 cups cooked white rice	2 cups boiled prawns
½ cup chopped celery	½ cup chopped capsicums
½ cup raw grated carrots	½ cup chopped parsley
½ cup french dressing	1 dsp gelatine
a few stuffed olives	a few strips pimento for garnishing
salt and freshly-ground pepper	1½ cups mayonnaise

Boil rice and cool. Melt gelatine in ¼ cup cold water and add to the mayonnaise. Add all the above chopped ingredients to the rice with seasonings; mix well, then mix

in mayonnaise and pour into a wet mould and keep in the refrigerator overnight. Unmould and garnish with a few large prawns, olives and pimento. Serve with french dressing or more mayonnaise.
Will serve eight to ten people.

QUENELLES DE POMFRET

2 large pomfrets	1 cup flour
3 eggs	½ tsp pepper,
1 tbsp prepared mustard	1 tsp salt
½ tsp mace powder	½ cup thick cream
1 cup butter	

Make quenelles one day before.

In a saucepan bring water to a boil with ¼ cup butter and 1 tsp salt. Add flour all at once, lower the heat, beat until it leaves the pan, about 2 min. Turn this mixture in a large bowl of the electric mixer and beat with the dough hook, add one egg at a time, beating well after each egg.

Fillet the pomfrets, wash them and dry on a paper towel or with a clean cloth, then pass through a meat grinder. Add this fish to the egg mixture and beat well, add all the seasonings and gradually beat in soft remaining butter and lastly the cream. Pour all this mixture in an oblong glass baking dish, refrigerate overnight.

Next day, make quenelles by shaping them into rolls of 2½ x 2".

In a large pan, pour 4 inches of water and bring it to a boil, place a few quenelles at a time in boiling water and cook, turning only once; when done, lift out with a slotted spoon and put in a serving dish; keep warm until all are done. Before serving, pour lobster or prawn sauce over it.

Lobster or Prawn Sauce:

3 cups prawns or lobster meat	2 tbsp flour
2 tbsp butter	2 egg yolks
1 cup thin cream	1 tsp salt
½ cup sherry	¼ tsp pepper

Melt butter add flour fry a little and add cream (milk can be used).

Stir over very low heat until it boils; add lobster or prawn meat, season with salt and pepper and a pinch of cayenne pepper. Just before serving heat the sauce, beat in egg yolks, cook for a minute, take it off the fire, add sherry and pour over the quenelles. Serve hot.

Lobster meat or prawns must be chopped very fine. Add a drop of red food colour to make the sauce slightly pink, or if liked add two tbsp of tomato ketchup. I prefer the colour, for ketchup changes the flavour.

This serves about 12-18 people.

STUFFED MULLET (BOI)

6 large mullets
3 dsp minced parsley
1 tbsp dill leaves chopped
½ cup butter
1 small tin mushrooms

6 dsp minced spring
onions
2 tbsp lemon juice
¼ cup chopped olives
salt and pepper

Clean mullets and slit them from one side, remove the centre bone, wash well and wipe with clean cloth.

Combine onions, parsley, dill, olives, sliced mushrooms, salt, pepper and lemon juice. Stuff each mullet with this mixture, secure with toothpicks, butter a shallow glass dish, lay all the mullet in it, put a dab of butter on each fish, cover with a lid or foil, bake for 20 min. Serve hot with slices of lemon. Mackerel fish can also be used.

LOBSTER AMERICANA

3 cups lobster meat
½ cup diced carrots
1 cup chopped tomatoes
½ cup butter
2 tbsp chopped parsley
1 cup fish stock
    made from the lobster
    shells
¼ cup salad oil

½ cup brandy or
1 cup white wine
2 onions finely chopped
6 slices finely chopped
garlic
¼ cup tomato puree
1 tsp salt
¼ tsp pepper, freshly
ground

Boil whole lobsters and remove meat. Melt salad oil in a pan and lightly fry the lobster in it, add a little salt and pepper and keep it aside. Melt butter in the same pan and saute chopped onion, garlic and carrots until soft; then add all the lobster meat with the other ingredients, except brandy and wine. Cook until ½ cup liquid remains. Pour wine or brandy over it just before serving. Serve with white rice.

Will serve six to eight people.

SPANISH PRAWNS

4 cups peeled prawns	6 large red ripe tomatoes
8 slices garlic	peeled, seeded and
4 tbsp butter	chopped finely
1 tsp chilli powder	6 bay leaves
1 cup water	2 tbsp chopped green
1 tbsp sugar	olives
2 tbsp chopped pimento	1 dsp salt and pepper
4 onions	freshly ground
4 tbsp salad oil	

Chop onions and garlic finely, saute in hot mixture of oil and butter until golden brown; add tomatoes and cook for 10 min; then add cleaned prawns, salt, pepper, chilli powder, sugar and ½ cup of water, cook until prawns are pink; add bay leaves, olives and pimento. Serve hot.

Will serve eight to ten people.

PRAWN ANDALUZIA

2 cups cooked prawns	¼ tsp pepper
3 onions cut into rings	3 red ripe tomatoes
½ cup white wine or	½ cup salad oil
cider vinegar	1 tbsp prepared mustard
1 tsp grated horse-radish	1" tsp chilli powder
1 dsp salt	1 dsp lemon juice

Combine all the above ingredients, except onion and tomatoes. Pour the mixture all over the cooked prawns and leave it in the refrigerator overnight.

54 PARTY RECIPES

Next day cut tomatoes and onions in rings. Take a glass dish and in the bottom arrange all the slices of tomatoes; drain prawns from the dressing and put a layer of it over the tomatoes, then a layer of onion rings, again a layer of prawns and onion rings. The last layer should be of onion rings. Pour all the drained dressing over the lot, chill and serve sprinkled with parsley before serving.

Will serve six to eight people.

PRAWNS IN CREOLE SAUCE

Sauce
2 cups cooked prawns
2 tbsp butter
2 cups chopped tomatoes
    peeled and seeded
1 dsp brown sugar
2 tbsp butter, salt, pepper

½ chopped spring onions
2 capsicums, chopped
1 tbsp chilli sauce
1 cup water
1 dsp salt
½ tsp pepper

Fry prawns lightly in butter; add salt and pepper and keep aside.

Make sauce by melting butter in a pan; add onions and fry until golden; add tomatoes, capsicums and water; simmer over slow fire until tomatoes are tender; add salt, pepper, sugar and chilli sauce; add prawns and simmer for another 5 min; add ¼ cup rum if liked; if preferred hot, add more chilli sauce.

Will serve eight to ten people.

TUNA OMELETTE

1 small tin tuna fish
1 small lettuce or a few
    spinach leaves
1 dsp lemon juice
½ tsp chopped ginger

6 eggs
1 small onion chopped
2 green chillies chopped
4 slices chopped garlic
salt and pepper

Shred the leaves, flake the tuna and mix with all the above ingredients. Whip eggs lightly with salt and pepper.

Heat oil in a large frying pan, lower the heat, put in the tuna mixture and spread well; over it pour the whipped eggs, close the lid of the pan, and cook on slow fire until the eggs are set, serve hot cut in pieces, with tomato ketchup.

Will serve six to eight people.

TUNA NEWBERG

2 cups fresh tuna or 2 tins tuna	3 egg yolks
½ tsp grated nutmeg	1 dsp salt
4 tbsp butter	¼ tsp pepper

Boil fish in very little water until cooked; flake it, melt butter in a pan; add cooked or tinned tuna and fry lightly for a while or until all liquid dries up. Add salt and pepper.

Beat cream and yolks lightly, and just before serving, add to fish mixture. Heat but do not boil; add 2 tbsp sherry or rum and serve on hot buttered or fried toasts.

Any other fish or shell fish can be used. This mixture can also be served in baked pastry shells.

Will serve six to eight people.

TUNA BAKE

1 large tin tuna fish	4 tbsp. butter
½ cup chopped mushrooms	½ cup chopped celery
½ cup chopped capsicum	1 cup cheddar cheese (grated)
4 eggs	2 cups milk
1 tsp mustard	2 tbsp chopped onion
1 cup bread cubes lightly fried in butter.	1 tsp salt
	¼ tsp pepper

Grease a baking dish and put a layer of tuna first, then a layer of chopped onions, mushrooms, celery and capsicum and ½ of the fried bread cubes. Cover all this with the remaining tuna and bread cubes.

Beat eggs with mustard, salt and pepper; add milk, pour over the tuna, sprinkle cheese on top and bake in a hot oven until set. Do not overbake, otherwise it will water.

Will serve six to eight people.

SALMON AND WALNUT BALL

1 tin pink salmon
1 cup cottage cheese,
    whipped to creamy
    consistency
1 dsp. chopped gherkins
½ cup chopped walnuts

2 tbsp minced onion
1 tbsp lemon juice
½ tsp salt
¼ tsp pepper
pinch of cayenne

Drain the salmon, remove the bones and flake it, combine with all other ingredients except walnuts. Chill overnight.

Mix 3 tbsp of chopped parsley with walnuts.

Shape the salmon mixture into a ball and roll in the walnut and parsley mixture. Chill for a few hours. Serve in a platter surrounded by melba toasts or crackers.

Will serve eight to ten people.

GRATIN OF ROE

1 pair of roe
3 tbsp flour
1 cup grated cheese
1 tbsp W. sauce
3 tbsp butter

2 cups milk
½ tsp mustard
¼ tsp tobasco, salt,
    pepper

Make cheese sauce by melting butter, add flour, fry a little; then add hot milk, stir until thick and smooth; add cheese and seasonings and keep it aside.

Grease a shallow pan with 1 tbsp butter, place in it cleaned and washed roe, sprinkle with salt and pepper and cover with greased paper and bake in a moderate oven for about 20 min. Remove from oven, and cool a little and then split each roe and stuff with the following stuffing, place in a greased serving dish, cover with cheese sauce, sprinkle some cheese over it and bake until the top is brown. Serve hot.

Stuffing:

1 small tin mushrooms
1 green chilli
½ cup cream
1 egg
¼ tsp chilli powder

1 onion
1 tbsp lemon juice
½ cup breadcrumbs
½ tsp salt
¼ tsp pepper

Chop mushrooms onion and chilli, finely mix with cream, breadcrumbs, salt, pepper and chilli powder; beat egg a little and mix in the mushroom mixture; add lemon juice.

A little more breadcrumbs may be needed if the mixture is very thin.

Will serve eight to ten people.

BAKED CRAB

6 large crabs
2 tbsp flour
½ tsp pepper
1 cup grated cheese
1 capsicum or green chilli
½ tsp mustard powder

4 tbsp butter
2 cups milk
½ tsp tobasco
2 eggs
2 tbsp tomato sauce
1 tsp salt

Clean crabs and chop the meat. Melt butter in a pan, add flour; fry a little, then add hot milk, stir until thick and creamy, add the rest of the ingredients, leaving a little cheese aside. Cool the mixture. Beat eggs a little and add to the above mixture; pour all this in a greased baking dish, sprinkle with cheese and bake in a hot oven until set. Serve hot.

This dish can be prepared and kept, and baked just before serving. The mixture can also be baked in crab shells.

Will serve six to eight people.

DEVILLED LOBSTERS

6 Lobsters (medium sized)	¼ tsp pepper
2 tbsp flour	4 tbsp butter
1 cup any fish stock	1 cup cream
1 tbsp chilli sauce	¼ tsp chilli powder
1 tbsp lemon juice	1 chopped onion ·
½ cup grated cheese	1 tsp sugar
1 dsp salt	3 slices of bread cut into cubes and dry fried

Boil lobsters, remove the meat and chop into pieces. Melt butter, add flour, fry a little, then add stock and cream, stir until thick and creamy; add onion lobster and seasonings; before baking, add fried croutons. Pour the mixture into a greased dish and sprinkle cheese over it. Bake in a hot oven until brown on top.

This mixture can also be baked in lobster shells.

To dryfry bread cubes, put 1 tbsp oil in a pan, add bread cubes and keep stirring until crisp.

Will serve six to eight people.

CHUTNEY-FILLED FISH ROLLS

2 large pomfrets	2-3 eggs
breadcrumbs	salt, oil for frying

Chutney:

6 green chillies	1 large bunch coriander
1 coconut	1 tsp cummin
1 tsp sugar	juice of 1 lemon
½ tsp salt	6 slices garlic, if liked

Grind all the above masala for the chutney, add lemon juice and keep it aside.

Fillet pomfrets, apply 2 tbsp salt and keep for ½ hour; then wash and cut each fillet into two crosswise, you will get 16 pieces; then lay each fillet flat on the board and with a very sharp knife slice into half but do not disjoin it, should be joined on the side, lay each piece flat and flatten with a knife, put a little chutney on each and roll up, and put a toothpick in each roll and make all the 16 rolls. Put it in the refrigerator. Just before serving, roll them in flour, then in beaten eggs and then in bread-crumbs; fry in deep hot oil, until crisp and golden. Drain on paper before serving.

These rolls can be also dipped in batter and fried, but must be served immediately.

Will serve eight to twelve people.

FISH ROLLS IN BORDELAIS SAUCE

2 large pomfrets	4 tbsp butter
2 tbsp flour	2 onions finely chopped
2 small tomatoes	1 cup cream
2 egg yolks	¼ tsp pepper
a few stuffed olives	¼ cup sherry or brandy
1 dsp salt	

Fillet pomfrets and make rolls as stated in *"Chutney-filled Fish Rolls"*, without the chutney, make 2 cups stock from the fish bones.

Melt butter and saute chopped onions until golden, then add flour and fry for a while; do not brown, then take it off the fire arrange fish rolls in it; (with tooth standing upright). Sprinkle with salt and pepper, add finely chopped tomatoes to it and one cup stock, put it on a slow fire; cover the pan and let it cook until the fish is cooked; do not stir, just lift the pan and shake it around, remove the picks, leave it until serving time.

Before serving, heat the fish, mix egg yolks and cream together, and add to the hot fish, cook for a little while, but do not boil; add sherry and serve, sprinkled with a few sliced olives or parsley.

Will serve eight to twelve people.

FISH SOUFFLE

2 cups dry boiled fish	2 cups milk
4 tbsp butter	4 tbsp flour
2 tbsp chopped spring onions	1 capsicum
1 tomato	1 dsp salt
4 eggs	½ tsp pepper

Melt butter, add flour, fry a little and add hot milk gradually, stir until thick, add chopped capsicum, onion and tomato; take it off the fire and add chopped boiled fish, salt and pepper; cool, beat in egg yolks, and then fold in stiffly-beaten egg whites. Pour in a greased baking dish and bake in a moderate oven until done.

Serve with the following sauce:

1 large pineapple tin	2 tbsp butter
2 tbsp flour	½ cup cream
½ tsp salt, pepper	1 dsp lemon juice

Drain pineapple and chop them finely. Melt butter add flour, fry for a while add p. juice and cream and keep stirring until the sauce is thick; add salt and pepper and chopped pineapple. Just before serving, add lemon juice.

Will serve ten to twelve people.

FISH IN ORANGE CREAM SAUCE

2 large pomfrets	2 tbsp butter
1 onion	2 tbsp flour
4 bay leaves	salt, pepper
8 peppercorns	1 tsp W. sauce
½ cup chopped celery	a few drops tobasco
2 cups orange juice	1 tsp sugar
2 tbsp finely sliced orange	1 cup cream
rind	2 egg yolks

Fillet pomfrets, place them in a pan (do not overlap them) with 1 cup water, ½ cup orange juice, sliced onion, bay leaves, celery, peppercorns and 1 tsp salt. Simmer over low heat until the fish is cooked, remove the fillets to a serving dish. Boil the stock to 1 cup, then strain.

Melt butter, add flour and fry a while, add 1 cup hot stock, then 1½ cups orange juice and rind, stir over low heat until it boils; add seasonings and sugar; keep aside until serving time.

Just before serving, heat the sauce, beat cream and egg yolks and add to the sauce, stir over low heat until thick, do not boil. Pour over the fish. Garnish with orange sections, a few capers or sliced olives, make a border of fried croutons cut in different shapes. Serve immediately. Any orange-flavoured liqueur may be added.

Will serve eight to ten people.

DRY BOMBAY DUCK TARAPORI PATIO

24 dry Bombay ducks	4 onions
½ cup sweet oil	1 tsp turmeric
2 cups vinegar	25 red chillies Goa
1 pod garlic	2 tsp cummin
2 tbsp jaggery	1 dsp salt

Clean the Bombay ducks, slit and remove the bone, wash well with water and then with a little vinegar, keep aside.

Grind chillies, cummin, turmeric, and garlic in vinegar to a fine paste. Roast onions in the oven until soft, then chop finely.

Heat oil and fry the masala in it. Add chopped onions and the Bombay duck, add salt and jaggery and the remaining vinegar, simmer on slow fire until oil floats on top.

Will serve ten to twelve people.

NARGOLI TARAPORI PATIO (VERY HOT)

50 Bombay ducks	100 gm chillie powder
100 gm dhanajeera	1 tbsp turmeric
50 gm cummin	2 pods garlic
1-1½ bottles vinegar	1 dsp salt

Clean Bombay ducks and cut into pieces, wash with vinegar.

Chop garlic, grind cummin in a little vinegar. Mix all the masala in vinegar with garlic and cummin, add Bombay duck and keep for an hour. Then add salt and the remaining vinegar to cover the Bombay ducks, cook on slow fire until dry.

This keeps for a very long time and can be served as pickle.

If a little sweetness is preferred, add some jaggery.

Will serve twenty to twenty-five people.

SWEET AND SOUR FISH SAUCE

8 fillets of fish
6 green chillies
10 slices garlic
2 tsp cummin
2 dsp sugar
1 bunch coriander

2 cups stock made from
    fish bones
3 red chillies
½ cup vinegar
½ cup oil, 1 dsp salt

Chop onions, chillies, garlic and coriander finely. Grind to a paste red chillies and cummin.

Heat oil and fry onions until golden, then add garlic and chillies, fry awhile, add chilli and cummin paste and fry for a while, then add fish stock and salt, bring to a boil, add fish fillet and simmer until fish is cooked.

Before serving, heat the fish. Beat 4 eggs lightly with vinegar and sugar, add to the fish and cook over slow fire, do not boil.

Serve sprinkled with chopped coriander; this is good served with yellow rice. If it is to be served with bread, add only 1 cup fish stock.

Will serve eight to ten people.

PRAWN KABABS (HOT)

2 cups fresh prawns
6 green chillies
1 tsp cummin
1 bunch coriander
1 tbsp vinegar
2 large eggs
4 large onions

6 slices garlic
1 dsp dhanajeera powder
1 tbsp gram flour
    (besan)
1 tsp sugar
1 dsp salt, oil for frying

Chop 2 onions finely and fry in a little oil until brown, drain from oil and keep aside. Chop coriander.

Grind 2 onions with chillies, garlic, cummin, dhanajeera, turmeric and prawns (raw) to a fine paste. Then add gram flour, vinegar, sugar and fried onions, mix all this with eggs. Form into small kababs and fry in hot oil, drain on paper, serve on picks for cocktails, or with plain dal and rice.

Will serve ten to twelve people.

FISH MASALA IN COCONUT MILK

8 fillets of pomfret	4 onions
6 red chillies	1 tsp cummin
4 cardamoms	½ tsp peppercorns
4 cloves	¼ nutmeg
½ tsp turmeric	1 small piece ginger
6 slices garlic	1 bunch coriander
½ coconut	1 dsp salt

Wash fillets, apply salt and keep them aside.

Grind finely all the above ingredients, except coconut, onions and coriander.

Grate coconut, add 2 cups hot water and squeeze out all milk.

Chop onions finely and fry in ¼ cup oil until brown; add the ground masala and fry for a while, then add the coconut milk and bring to a boil, wash the fish and add; simmer on slow fire until the fish is cooked and the gravy is thick; add 1 tbsp of lemon juice.

Serve sprinkled with chopped coriander.

Will serve eight to ten people.

SWEET AND SOUR FISH PATIA

2 large pomfrets or any other fish cut into pieces	½ cup sweet oil
	6 red chillies
	½ pod garlic
2 tbsp gram flour	1 tbsp dry coriander
6 green chillies	(dhania)
1 dsp cummin	6 onions
1 bunch fresh coriander	2 tbsp jaggery
1 tbsp tamarind	1 dsp salt

Cut fish into pieces, wash and apply a little salt and keep it aside. Grind chillies, garlic, cummin, dry coriander and 3 onions finely. Heat oil and fry 3 finely chopped onions until brown; then add the masala and fry well; add salt and jaggery and fry awhile, then add gram flour, fry, and add 2 cups water, bring it to a boil. Wash the fish and add to the masala with tamarind water, and chopped coriander. Cook on slow fire until fish is cooked and oil floats on top.

Serve with yellow rice or khichree.

A few green chillies may be added, if preferred hot. *Will serve eight to ten people.*

TARAPORI FISH PATIA

8 fillets of pomfrets	15 red chillies
10 green chillies	1 pod garlic
1 tbsp cummin	1 tsp turmeric
1 tbsp sambhar or	3 onions
dhanajeera	3 tbsp jaggery
¾ cup sweet oil	vinegar
1 dsp salt	

After filleting the pomfrets, make stock from the head and all the bones, by adding 3 cups of water and boiling until 2 cups remain, strain and keep aside.

Grind chillies, garlic, cummin and onions in vinegar to a fine paste. Heat oil and fry the masala in it, then add turmeric and sambhar and salt, fry well, then add jaggery and fry until jaggery melts, take it off the fire, add fish fillets, stir well, then pour in about ½ bottle of vinegar or until it just covers the fish. Leave aside for ½ hour. Then add the fish stock (2 cups if you want the patia served with rice, or just one cup). Put it on fire and bring it to a boil, then simmer on slow fire until the fish is cooked and oil floats on top; do not stir the fish, just lift the pan and shake it around. For this, take a shallow pan.

Will serve ten to twelve people.

PRAWN AND POMFRET MOUSSE

1 packet lemon jelly	8 fillets of pomfret
2 cups boiled prawns	1 small onion
2 cloves	2 sprigs of parsley
1/4 tsp mace	1 tsp salt, pepper
2 tbsp butter	2 tbsp flour
1 cup milk	1/2 cup cream
1 tsp tobasco	1 dsp W. sauce
1 tbsp lemon juice	

Melt lemon jelly in a cup of hot water.

Put fish fillets, bones from the fish. onion, cloves, parsley, mace, salt and pepper in a pan with 1 cup water or a little more to cover the fish; close the lid and bring to a boil; then simmer until the fish is cooked, remove the fillets and strain the stock and keep aside about 1 cup; if more, boil it down to a cup.

Melt butter add flour, brown a little, add hot milk and cook the sauce until thick; to this add fillets and boiled prawns (keeping a few aside for garnish). Add tobasco, W. sauce, lemon juice and blend all until smooth. Add lemon jelly and blend again, remove and add cream. Pour into a wet mould and chill overnight.

Unmould and garnish with prawns, boiled eggs and lettuce.

Will serve twelve to fifteen people.

FRESH SARDINES IN MASALA

2 doz. sardines	6 slices garlic
1/2 tsp turmeric	6 green chillies
3 onions	1 piece ginger
chopped coriander	salt, oil

Clean sardines and keep whole, wash, drain and apply 1 tbsp salt and turmeric and keep it for 30 min.

Heat 3 tbsp oil and fry chopped onion until golden; then add chopped ginger and garlic; then add sardines, and chopped chillies and 1/2 cup water. Cook over low heat until fish is cooked. Serve hot, sprinkled with coriander leaves and some sliced lemon.

Will serve six to eight people.

POMFRETS STUFFED WITH MASALA

Two large pomfrets cleaned and slit on one side for the masala.

Grind in vinegar 10 red Goa chillies, 1 tsp cummin seeds, 6 peppercorns, 1 piece ginger, 6 slices garlic, 1 tsp turmeric, 1 tbsp jaggery, 1 tsp tamarind, 1 dsp salt.

Apply salt to the pomfret and keep aside; after 1 hour, apply the ground masala to the whole fish, put some masala in the slit. Heat some oil in a fry pan and fry pomfrets in it on slow fire. Serve hot with lemon slices.

Will serve six to eight people.

FISH FILLETS IN GRAVY

8 *fillets of pomfrets or*	6 *slices garlic*
any white fish sliced	4 *red chillies*
3 *onions*	½ *tsp turmeric*
6 *green chillies*	*juice of 1 lemon*
1 *dsp cummin*	1 *dsp salt, ¼ cup sweet*
1 *bunch coriander*	*oil*
4 *large tomatoes*	

Grind red chillies, cummin and turmeric and apply to the fish.

Chop onions, green chillies, gàrlic. Wash tomatoes and chop fine.

Heat oil and fry the fish in it on both sides, remove from oil and keep aside; in the same oil fry onions brown; then add chopped chillies, garlic and tomatoes and ½ cup water, bring to a boil, then place fried fish in it and simmer until the fish is cooked and the gravy is thick. Add lemon juice and serve, sprinkled with coriander.

Will serve eight to ten people.

TUNA OR SALMON PATE

1 tin tuna or salmon (1 lb.)	1 tbsp lemon juice
6 tbsp salad oil	1 tbsp gelatine
½ cup soft butter	1½ tsp mustard powder
2 tbsp minced onion	2 tbsp brandy or sherry
1 tsp salt and pepper	a few drops tobasco

Flake tuna and remove bones, if any; to this add all the other ingredients including soft butter and gelatine which is dissolved in very little hot water. Blend all in a blender until smooth.

Grease and line the bottom of a square pan with some salad oil.

Then pour the mixture in it. Chill overnight, unmould on a platter and garnish with olives and some sliced tomatoes.

Will serve ten to twelve people.

ROE MOUSSE

1 large pair roe	juice of 2 lemons
1 tsp mustard powder	2 tbsp cider vinegar
½ cup mayonnaise	2 dsp W. sauce
1 cup cream	a few drops tobasco
2 tbsp gelatine	1 dsp castor sugar
1 tsp salt and pepper	

Clean the roe and add 1 cup water and salt about 1 dsp and cook on slow fire until cooked. Soak gelatine in a little cold water, then add to the hot roe liquid. Cut roe in small pieces and blend it with the liquid to which the gelatine is added. Add all other ingredients except cream and blend again, remove from the blender and fold in cream. Pour into a greased and lined pan and chill overnight. Unmould and garnish.

Will serve twelve to fifteen people.

PRAWN AND EGG BAKE

¼ kilo cleaned prawns	6 hardboiled eggs
1 cup grated cheese	2 cups milk
2 dsp flour	1 tsp salt, ¼ tsp pepper
1 tsp mustard powder	¼ tsp chilli powder
2 tbsp butter	¼ cup chopped parsley

Boil prawns in very little water until it turns pink.

Make sauce by melting butter in a pan, add flour, brown a little, then add hot milk gradually, stirring continuously until sauce thickens and comes to a boil; take it off the fire and add cheese, keeping some aside; add seasonings.

Butter a pie dish, lay the prawn in the bottom, over it put sliced hardboiled eggs, sprinkle parsley over it and then cover all with cheese sauce; sprinkle with cheese and bake in a hot oven for about 20 min or until browned on top. Serve hot.

Will serve six to eight people.

PUNGENT PRAWNS

4 cups boiled prawns	2 tbsp cornflour
6 spring onions	2 large capsicums
½ cup brown sugar	1 tbsp soya sauce
1 large tin pineapple slices	½ cup vinegar, 1 tsp salt

Drain the pineapple juice and to it add sugar, soya sauce, vinegar and cornflour; cook all this over slow fire until thick. Cut pineapple into pieces, cut capsicums and onions into thick slices, add all this to the above sauce and cook for a minute. Just before serving, add prawns and heat. Serve with rice or boiled noodles.

A little sherry may be added, if desired.

Will serve six to eight people.

PRAWN PATE

2½ cups shelled prawns
2 tbsp gelatine
1½ cups mayonnaise
2 tsp lemon juice
1 tsp salt, pepper
a few drops tobasco
6 spring onions minced

¼ cup brandy or sherry
½ cup cream
1 tbsp W. sauce
4-5 drops Angustura
  bitters
a few drops cocheanal

Clean the prawns and cook in ¼ cup water until pink, about 5 min, do not overcook. Add salt and gelatine, stir until gelatine melts, then add all the above ingredients and blend in a blender until smooth. Colour a very delicate pink, add the cocheanal drop by drop. Taste for salt, pour the mixture in an 8"x8" square pan which is very lightly oiled and chilled. Leave overnight to set in the refrigerator.

Unmould on a platter and garnish with prawns, olives or any other garnish.

Soak gelatine in a little cold water and then add to the hot prawns.

This dish makes a nice buffet party dish and will serve about 12-18 people. If served as a first course, then it will do for 12 people.

PICKLED PRAWNS

3 cups shelled prawns
¾ cup salad oil
12 bay leaves
1 tsp mustard powder
2 tbsp castor sugar
6 medium white onions
½ cup lemon juice

1 cup cider vinegar
1 tsp freshly ground
  pepper
½ tsp chilli powder
2 tsp salt
2 tbsp chopped corian-
  der

Boil prawns without water, keep turning them in the pan until pink, do not overcook. Peel and slice onions into rings.

Heat salad oil in a pan, add prawns and simmer until the water evaporates, take it off fire, add all the seasonings, then layer in a glass bowl, one layer prawns and one layer onion rings, until all is used up. Pour hot salad oil over it (oil in which prawns were simmered). Chill overnight. Toss before serving, put in a serving bowl and sprinkle coriander leaves over it.

Will serve ten to twelve people.

FRESH ROE SALAD

1 pair roe
6 slices garlic
½ cup salad oil
4 drops tobasco
4 large slices white bread

a few chopped olives
6 spring onions minced
2 tbsp lemon juice
1 tbsp chopped parsley
1 tsp salt and pepper

Boil the roe in some water and drain the water off. Trim crusts from the bread and soak in water, after a while squeeze the water out and add to the roe, add salt and blend in a blender until smooth; add all the other ingredients except parsley and olives and blend again. Pour the mixture in a glass bowl and chill. Sprinkle sliced olives and parsley before serving.

Serve with melba toasts, as a first course.

Will serve ten to twelve people.

PICKLED SARDINES

3 cups cleaned whole fresh sardines
12 peppercorns
6 bay leaves
½ cup cider vinegar
2 medium white onions

1 dsp salt
1 cup salad oil
1 tsp ginger powder
juice of 2 lemons
4 slices garlic

Clean fish and sprinkle with salt and lemon juice and keep for 2 hours. Then drain the liquid off. Heat the salad oil and simmer the fish in it for 15 min. over slow fire. Remove fish to a bowl. To the hot oil, add all the other ingredients with sliced onion rings and garlic, toss well and pour over the fish; when cool refrigerate chill 24 hours before serving. It can be served as hors-d'oeuvres.

Will serve eight to ten people.

POULTRY

Poultry is no longer a special occasion dish, and as so many poultry farms have cropped up all over the country, Indian chickens are fast disappearing and broilers are taking their place. The Indian chicken's flavour might be a bit better, but the broilers are as good and definitely more meaty.

Poultry now is more or less on par with other meats and, therefore, can be used more often in family dinners.

Fresh chicken will of course taste best, but frozen ones can be used as successfully.

A frozen bird must be thawed completely before using, left out and brought to room temperature. Do not soak it in water—it loses a lot of its flavour.

If you buy a live bird, it must be plucked and drawn immediately on purchase.

Chickens are deceptive—inspect them carefully before buying. They must be fresh-looking and pinky, the skin must be moist and the flesh soft. Do not buy a chicken that is hard and dark in colour.

Capons are young male birds—they are used for roasting, or are boiled and the flesh removed for making mousse or salad.

The best broilers are a kilo each, or a little more. Very big birds are good for boiling and the flesh is used for making mousses and mincing for croquettes and souffles.

BUFFET CHICKEN

2 chickens
½ pkt fine noodles
1 cup corn
4 chopped tomatoes
4 sliced capsicums
2 sliced onions
1 cup sliced celery

½ cup chopped olives
(green or black)
1 cup grated cheese
½ cup salad oil
1 tsp curry powder
1 dsp salt and pepper

Boil chicken until tender, leaving 3 cups stock. Bone the chicken and cut into small pieces.

Boil noodles in 3 cups chicken stock; if required, add a little water. If using frozen corn, give it a boil in water and drain.

Heat ½ cup salad oil, add onions, celery, and capsicums, and fry until tender. Do not brown. Add tomatoes, curry powder, and cook until liquid dries up. Then add to it noodles, chicken, corn and season with salt and pepper. Add olives, mix all together and pour into a baking dish. Sprinkle with cheese. This can be kept ready. Before serving, put the dish for about 30 min. in a moderate oven until the cheese melts. Serve hot.

Will serve six to eight people.

CHICKEN IN JELLY

1 to 1½ kg chicken
2 tbsp gelatine
1 cup thinly sliced carrot
1 cup thinly sliced
onions

3 bay leaves
3 slices garlic
2 tbsps chopped parsley
1 dsp salt and pepper
¼ cup sherry or rum

Boil chicken in four cups water with salt, garlic, bay leaves and a small piece of ginger.

When the chicken is cooked, remove from stock, debone it, and slice the meat. Chill the stock (about 2 cups), remove the fat from the top, then add one whole egg with shell (crushed) and boil the stock until it is clear. Strain through a muslin cloth, add gelatine which has been soaked in a little cold water. Stir until gelatine melts, taste for salt, add a little pepper or tobasco sauce. Parboil carrots and onion slices, add salt. Chop parsley.

In a square pan, layer slices of chicken with slices of carrot and onions, sprinkle parsley in between each layer and pour gelatine stock of tomatoes and hardboiled eggs. Serve with lettuce leaves.

Will serve six to eight people.

CHICKEN AND CORN CASSEROL

2 Chickens
½ cup chopped onion
6 bay leaves
¼ cup chopped olives
1 can kernels
2 tbsp flour
½ tsp chilli powder
2 tbsp W. sauce
few drops of tobasco

½ cup chopped celery
¼ cup chopped capsicum
½ kilo skinned and chopped tomatoes
6 slices garlic
¼ tsp sago
1 dsp salt, pepper each
2 dsp sugar
¼ cup butter

Cut chicken pieces add celery, bay leaves and salt, add enough water to cover the chicken, simmer until tender. Remove the chicken from gravy and debone the pieces. Strain the gravy.

Melt butter and saute the onions' and capsicum until tender (5 min.) stir in flour, tomatoes and seasonings, stir until smooth; add chicken and cook for a while, then add olives.

Butter a baking dish, arrange in it ½ corn, ¼ chicken and pour half the sauce, repeat the three layers again. Sprinkle with breadcrumbs and bake for 30 min. Serve hot.

Use gherkin instead of olives, if liked. Packet corn can be used but give it one boil in hot water before using.

Will serve six to eight people.

MOULDED CHICKEN WITH CURRY SAUCE

2 large chickens
4 cloves
8 peppercorns
1 piece cinnamon
1 dsp salt
2 slightly beaten egg
    whites
few thin slices of capsi-
    cum or pimento

1 tbsp sugar
½ cup chopped celery
½ cup chopped carrots
½ cup chopped onions
6 bay leaves
3 dsp gelatine powder
2 tbsp lemon juice
12 stuffed olives

Boil chicken with celery, carrots, onion, cloves, pepper-corn, cinnamon, bay leaves, salt and six cups of water, until chicken is tender. Strain the stock (about two cups of stock should remain).

Soak gelatine in a little cold water and add to the hot stock with egg whites; bring to a boil and then strain, add lemon juice and sugar. Keep in the refrigerator until it jells a little. Arrange sliced olives and capsicum in the bottom of the mould, pour a little gelatine stock and let it set.

Debone chickens, cut breasts into slices, chop the rest of the chicken. Arrange the breast slices over the set olives and capsicum, mix the remaining chicken with the gelatine stock, pour all this in the mould and set well.

Unmould on a platter, garnish with hardboiled eggs, tomatoes and radish roses. Serve with curry sauce.

Curry Sauce:

2 cups mayonnaise
¼ cup tomato ketchup
1 tbsp W. sauce

1 tbsp lemon juice
2 rounded tsp curry
    powder

Mix all and chill well. Curry powder may be adjusted to taste.

Will serve twelve to sixteen people.

CHICKEN AND WALNUT MOULD

3 cups cooked chicken
   pieces
1 cup chicken stock
½ cup chopped walnuts
½ cup cream
1 dsp sugar
¼ cup cold water

1 cup mayonnaise
2 tbsp sherry
2 dsp gelatine powder
½ cup chopped celery
¼ cup chopped olives
salt and pepper to taste

Mix gelatine in cold water, add to the hot chicken
stock, add sugar and cool; add mayonnaise, sherry, salt,
pepper and all the other ingredients. Pour into a chilled
mould and set overnight.

Unmould and garnish. Serve with mayonnaise.

Will serve ten to twelve people.

CHICKEN MOUSSE WITH PINEAPPLE

3 cups cooked chicken
   pieces
3 dsp gelatine
1 cup mayonnaise
½ cup finely chopped
   spring onion
½ cup chopped toasted
   almonds, or cashew
   nuts

a few drops tobasco
1 can cream of chicken
   soup
1 tbsp. lemon juice
1 cup cream
½ cup chopped celery
1 big can pineapple

Mix gelatine in ¼ cup pineapple juice, add to cream
of chicken soup, and bring to boil, stir until gelatine melts,
cool, add the seasonings, chicken and all other ingredients,
mix well, leave aside 4 slices of pineapple and chop the
rest, add to the chicken mixture. Pour all this in a wet
oiled mould, and chill overnight.

Unmould on lettuce leaves, arrange ½ slices of pineapple around it, garnish with radish roses. Serve with
mayonnaise.

Will serve ten to twelve people.

ROAST CHICKEN WITH ORANGE FLAMBE

2 chickens
4 bay leaves
6 peppercorns
4 tbsp butter
½ cup orange juice

2 tbsp honey
1 tbsp orange rind, fine-
  ly chopped
1 dsp salt

Wash chickens and leave them whole, make one cup stock from the neck and giblets or any odd pieces of chicken available.

Apply salt and pepper to the chickens and place them in a roasting pan. Mix orange juice, honey, orange rind and melted butter.

Roast the chicken in a moderate oven, basting the chickens with the orange honey mixture. If it gets very brown on top, lay a piece of foil over it. When the chicken is tender, remove the flesh from the bones in big pieces and place them on a platter, keep warm, just before serving garnish with orange sections. Flambe with ¼ cup brandy or rum, and serve with the following sauce:

Orange Sauce:

1 cup orange juice
1 tbsp grated orange
  rind
2 dsp cornflour
¼ cup brandy or rum

1 cup chicken stock (any
  gravy from the chicken
  can be strained and
  added)
⅛ tsp salt

Mix cornflour in a little orange juice. Mix chicken stock, orange juice, and rind, add cornflour and cook over slow fire, stirring until thick. Remove from fire add brandy or rum and serve hot.

Will serve six to eight people.

SHREDDED CHICKEN MOULD

1 chicken
2 tbsp chopped spring
  onions
6 eggs
1 tbsp soya sauce

½ cup butter
2 tbsp chopped capsi-
  cums
½ cup milk
1 tsp salt and pepper

Boil the chicken and remove meat in shreds. Melt butter and fry onions until golden; then add capsicums and shredded chicken and fry until chicken is also a little brown. Season with soya sauce, salt and pepper. Remove from fire and cool.

Beat eggs lightly with ½ cup milk. Then add to the chicken mixture. Pour all this into a greased bowl, put the bowl in hot water and steam until the mixture is set. Do not overcook. Invert the mould on a platter and serve hot with vegetables.

Will serve six to eight people.

CHICKEN BAKED WITH RICE

2 chickens
1 cup chopped onions
1 cup chopped celery
1 dsp salt
1 tsp pepper
½ tsp mixed herbs (oregano, rosemary or basil)

½ cup Delhi rice
6 slices garlic
3 cups of any stock (chicken, beef or mutton)
¼ tsp monosodium glutamate

Cut chicken into pieces, using only good pieces. Stock can be made out of odd pieces. Roast rice in a pan over low heat until brown, turning frequently.

Dredge chicken with seasoned flour and fry the pieces in hot oil until brown. Remove chicken from the oil, and in the same oil fry onions and minced garlic until golden. Then add rice, celery, herbs and seasonings. Mix well, put all this in a greased baking dish; top with chicken pieces, pour two cups of stock over it. Cover with lid or foil, and bake in a moderate oven for an hour. Remove the lid and check if rice and chicken are done; if not, add more stock until rice and chicken are done. Sprinkle with parsley and serve in the same dish.

Will serve eight to ten people.

FRICASSEE OF CHICKEN

2 chickens
¼ cup sliced carrots
1 kilo small white
 onions
¼ cup butter
½ tsp grated nutmeg
½ tsp chilli powder
1 cup cream

1 dsp salt and pepper
1 cup chopped onions
1 cup mushrooms
6 bay leaves
2 tbsp flour
½ tsp mace powder
2 tbsp chopped parsley
¼ cup sherry or rum

Cut chickens into pieces. Apply salt, pepper and chilli powder and saute in butter until golden. Add chopped onions, carrots, bay leaves and three cups of water, and cook the chicken until tender. Remove chicken to a casserole. Strain the gravy.

Melt butter and fry the whole onions to golden brown. Remove and fry the mushrooms in the same butter. All this to be added to the chicken casserole. Blend flour with the strained gravy; add to it nutmeg, mace, cream and salt. Pour all this over the chicken. Bake the casserole, covered for 30 min. Garnish with parsley.

Will serve six to eight people.

ORANGE CHICKEN WITH ALMONDS

1 chicken
½ cup butter
1 tsp salt
¼ tsp pepper

1 cup orange juice
½ cup sliced and toasted
 almonds

Cut chicken into pieces, apply salt and pepper, and fry until golden brown. Add 2 cups water, and let it cook until chicken is tender, and all the gravy has dried up. Remove chicken to a serving dish; in the butter that's remaining in the pan add orange juice, let it boil for a minute, then pour over the chicken and sprinkle with toasted almonds. Slices of oranges may be used for garnishing the dish. Serve with a mixed salad.

Will serve four to six people.

ROAST CHICKEN WITH RICE STUFFING

1 large chicken	4 large onions
4 tomatoes	1 cup chicken stock
¾ cup rice	3 green chillies
2 hardboiled eggs	¼ tsp chilli powder
12 medium-size	1 dsp salt and pepper
potatoes, parboiled	oil for frying
and peeled	

Clean chicken, wash and dry well with a towel. Chop the liver and giblet into small pieces. Chop onions, tomatoes and chillies. Melt two tbsp oil and fry onions to golden brown. Remove from oil and add washed rice to the pan. Fry rice for a while, then add tomatoes, chillies and one cup stock, let rice cook over slow fire until tender. A little more stock or water may be required. Remove from the fire and add fried onions and chopped hardboiled eggs. Season well with salt and pepper.

Fill the chicken with rice mixture and sew up opening.

Heat 4 tbsp oil in a big pan, and fry the chicken until it is brown all over. Then add 2 cups water and cook over slow fire until chicken is tender; 10 minutes before, it is cooked, add potatoes to it.

Serve the whole chicken on a platter, surrounded by potatoes. Serve gravy separately, and if the rice stuffing remains, serve separately.

Will serve four to six people.

BAKED BARBECUE CHICKEN

2 chickens	3 onions
1 cup water	salt and pepper

Cut chicken into pieces, slice onions into rings, grease well a baking dish, lay the onion rings on it, over it lay the chicken pieces, pour water, and bake in a moderate oven until chicken is half-cooked; then pour the following sauce over it and bake until chicken is tender. Baste the chicken frequently with the sauce. If there is too much liquid in the chicken, before pouring the sauce drain the liquid off, leaving only ½ cup liquid in the pan.

Sauce:

1 cup tomato juice	½ cup tomato ketchup
1 tbsp chilli sauce	1 tsp mustard powder
2 tbsp W. sauce	¼ cup vinegar
6 bay leaves	2 tbsp brown sugar
6 slices chopped garlic	1 tbsp lemon juice
1 tsp salt	½ tsp pepper

Mix all the above ingredients and bring to a boil. Simmer for 5 min, then baste the chicken with the sauce, until it is all over.

Chilli sauce may be adjusted according to taste.

Will serve six to eight people.

DUCK CASSEROLE

2 ducks	1 tbsp W. sauce
¼ kilo bacon	½ cup butter
2 tbsp chopped parsley	6 bay leaves
4 cups chicken stock	6 spring onions
(any other stock will	2 doz small white onions
do)	1 dsp salt and pepper
1 kilo green peas	

Cut ducks into pieces, apply salt and pepper and fry in butter until brown. Remove the pieces to a casserole. In the remaining butter, brown the chopped spring onions, then add chopped bacon and brown. Then add parsley, bay leaves and stock. Bring all this to a boil, simmer for 5 min, then pour over the duck pieces. Cover the casserole and bake for one hour in a moderate oven, then add to it peeled white onions. Close the casserole and bake further until duck is tender. Mix about 1 tbsp of flour with a little cold water to a smooth paste; then add to the casserole and mix well. Add W sauce, cook until sauce thickens. Boil the green peas and add to the casserole.

Will serve eight to ten people.

CHICKEN IN BREAD BASKET

1 medium loaf of bread, unsliced	1 chicken
2 large onions	6 slices garlic
1 piece ginger	2 tomatoes
2 dsp chopped coriander	2 tbsp W. sauce
¼ tsp chilli powder	2 tsp sugar
2 tbsp oil or butter	1 tsp salt and pepper

Boil chicken, remove the bones and cut into small pieces. Keep one cup stock aside. Melt 2 tbsp butter and fry chopped onions until golden, add chopped ginger, garlic and tomatoes, mix well, then add chicken and 1 cup stock. Cook for 5 min, until very little gravy remains. Add salt, pepper, coriander and W. sauce. Mix 2 tsp cornflour in a little water and add to the chicken mixture. Stir until thick.

Cut a slice from the top of the bread, then scoop out the soft bread from inside. Fry the bread case in oil, on all sides, then drain on paper to remove all oil.

Fill this bread case with the chicken mixture and garnish with slices of tomatoes, hardboiled eggs, green peas and parsley.

Serve hot.

Will serve four to six people.

LEMON CHICKEN

1 chicken	4 spring onions
2 tomatoes	1 tbsp chopped parsley
½ cup chopped celery	½ cup chopped carrots
1 onion	1 dsp salt and pepper

Cut chicken into pieces, put in a pan with all the chopped vegetables, onion, salt and pepper. Add four cups water and let it simmer until chicken is tender. Remove the chicken pieces to a platter, and strain the stock, which should be about 1½ cups.

Lemon Sauce:

2 tbsp butter	*½ tsp grated nutmeg*
1 tbsp flour	*2 tbsp lemon juice*
1½ cups chicken stock	*½ tsp lemon rind*
2 egg yolks	*1 tbsp capers*
½ cup cream	

Melt butter, add flour, fry awhile, then add the hot stock and stir until thick. Beat yolks and cream together, and add to the above mixture. Stir over slow fire, do not boil, take it off fire, add lemon juice, rind, nutmeg and capers. Pour all over the chicken pieces. If liked, half cup mushrooms can be used in the sauce. Surround the chicken with white rice or mashed potato.

Will serve four to six people.

DUCK IN ORANGES

1 large duck	*½ cup orange juice*
6 oranges, peeled and sliced	*1 tsp salt*
2 dsp minced orange peel (pith to be removed)	*¼ tsp pepper*
	2 tbsp butter
	½ cup sweet vermouth

Clean and wash duck.

Remove seeds from the sliced oranges, fill the duck full with oranges. Place on a roasting pan, pour orange juice over it and sprinkle with orange peel, put dabs of butter over the duck, and roast in a moderate oven. When cooked, remove to a platter, add vermouth to the gravy, and pour over the duck.

Serve with orange sections.

Rum can be used instead of vermouth.

Will serve four to six people.

DUCK STUFFED WITH PRUNES

1 large duck
¼ kilo prunes
½ cup breadcrumbs
½ cup chopped celery
1 cup apple cubes

¼ cup chopped capsicum
¼ cup orange juice
½ cup melted butter
1 tsp salt and pepper

Clean and wash the duck, pat it dry with a cloth.

Combine breadcrumbs, pitted and chopped prunes, apple, celery, capsicum, salt, pepper and orange juice (a little more orange juice may be needed if stuffing is dry). Stuff the duck with the mixture, place on a buttered pan, and brush the duck with melted butter. Bake in a moderate oven for about 2 hours, or until done. Baste once or twice again with melted butter.

Will serve four to six people.

DRY DUCK CURRY

1 large duck
2 tbsp dhania
2 tbsp poppy seeds
1 tsp mustard seeds
1 tsp cummin
6 red chillies
1 dsp sugar

1 tsp turmeric
1 piece ginger
6 slices garlic
3 onions
3 green chillies
¼ cup vinegar
1 dsp salt

Chop onions, ginger, garlic and green chillies.

Grind to a paste red chillies with roasted dhania, poppy seeds, mustard, cummin and turmeric.

Cut duck into pieces. Heat 3 tbsp oil in a pan and fry the pieces of duck until golden brown. In another pan heat 2 tbsp oil and fry onions until brown, then add ginger, garlic and green chillies. Fry for a while, then add the ground masala and fry well, until all the water evaporates then add duck pieces, mix well. Add 2 cups hot water and let it simmer over slow heat. Close the pan with the lid. When the duck is tender and all the water has dried up, add vinegar and sugar, mix well.

Serve with white rice and plain dal, or chapatis.

Will serve four to six people.

STUFFED BONELESS CHICKEN

1 large chicken
¼ kilo sausages
¼ kilo bacon
2 large slices bread
2 onions
2 slices garlic
2 tbsps chopped walnuts

2 tbsps chopped dried
  apricots
salt and pepper
2 dsps W. sauce
a few drops tobasco
one egg

Wash the chicken, slit the back and debone it. Then stitch the back again.

Chop bacon, remove the skin from the sausages (or use skinless sausages). Soak bread in ¼ cup milk, chop garlic and onions.

Mix sausages, bacon, garlic, onion, mashed bread, salt, pepper, walnuts, apricots, W. sauce and tobasco. Mix all well and add one egg to it. Fill the stuffing in the chicken and apply some butter all over it. Put it in a roasting pan and bake until done.

Serve in slices, with any vegetables or potato chips.
Will serve six to eight people.

CHICKEN STUFFED WITH RICE

1 large chicken
½ cup cooked rice
¼ kilo ham
¼ cup raisins or currants
¼ cup sliced almonds or
  cashewnuts
2 tbsp butter

1 tbsp lemon juice
½ tsp grated nutmeg
½ tsp all spice powder
¼ cup melted butter
salt and pepper
¼ cup sherry or any
  sweet wine

Wash the chicken and leave it whole. Melt butter and fry, sliced almonds to golden brown, then add raisins or currants and fry a little. To the cooked rice add chopped ham, fried almonds and raisins and all the seasoning. Mix well and stuff chicken with it. Put the chicken in a buttered pan, combine ¼ cup butter with lemon juice and sherry and brush the chicken with this mixture.   Roast in a moderate oven, basting with the butter mixture, until it is all over.

Serve hot.

Will serve four to six people.

CHICKEN CHAUDEFROID ON TOMATO RICE

1 large chicken	3 cloves
1 carrot	6 peppercorns
1 onion	2 blades of mace
1 potato	4 cups water
3 bay leaves	1 dsp salt

Boil chicken with chopped carrot, potato, onion, bay leaves, peppercorns, cloves, mace and salt, with 4 cups water.   Let it simmer in a covered pan until chicken is tender, remove from stock, skin it and when cool, cut into pieces, carefully removing the bone.   Chill.

Sauce:

1 tbsp butter	¾ cup chicken stock
1 tbsp flour	(left after the chicken
1 dsp gelatine	is boiled)
1 cup cream	½ cup finely chopped
salt	mushrooms
1 dsp lemon juice	

Melt butter, add flour and chicken stock, and stir smooth.   Add mushrooms and stir until thick, remove and blend in a blender and strain through a coarse sieve. Melt gelatine in ¼ cup water and add to the sauce.   Cool thoroughly, then add cream which has been whipped.

Tomato Rice:

1 cup long-grained raw rice	1 dsp sugar
3 cups tomato juice	salt and pepper

Bring the juice to a boil, add rice, salt, pepper and sugar, and let it cook until done. Cook it, then spread the rice on a serving platter, lay the cold chicken pieces over it, and spoon the sauce over the chicken.
Will serve six to eight people.

BAKED CHICKEN BREASTS

6 chicken breasts
¼ cup lemon juice
½ tsp chilli powder
½ tsp pepper
breadcrumbs

2 cups light cream
2 tbsp W. sauce
2 tsp salt
½ cup butter

Combine cream, lemon juice, W. sauce and seasonings.

Cut chicken breasts in half and wipe dry, add the pieces to the cream marinade and leave in the refrigerator overnight.

Next day take each piece with a little marinade on it and roll them in breadcrumbs, lay on a flat baking dish in single layer, spread half of the butter (melted) over the chicken pieces and bake in a moderate oven until the chicken is done, spoon the rest of the butter and bake for another 10 minutes.

Serve immediately.
Will serve six people.

BREAST OF CHICKEN WITH HOLLANDAISE SAUCE

4 chicken breasts
1 cup mushrooms
2 tbsp flour

1 cup chicken stock
1 cup light cream
¼ cup butter

Cut chicken breasts into two pieces, parboil them adding 1dsp salt and 2 cups water (some chicken bones may be added), when done 1 cup stock should remain, strain the stock and debone the breasts.

Melt butter in a pan and fry the pieces of chicken lightly in it, remove the chicken pieces, and in the same butter fry sliced mushrooms, remove the mushrooms, and add flour, then add chicken stock and cream, cook, stirring, until thick. Place breasts in the sauce and simmer until its cooked. When its cooked, add mushrooms, salt, and ¼ cup sherry to it, lay the chicken on a serving platter, spread the Hollandaise sauce over it and put the platter under a grill to brown the top. Serve immediately.

Will serve four people.

Hollandaise Sauce:

2 egg yolks
¼ cup melted butter
1 tbsp lemon juice

salt, pepper, pinch of
    cayenne pepper

Combine melted butter and lemon juice. In a bowl beat yolks until thick, add seasonings, then add melted butter, one tsp at a time, beating constantly until thick. Refrigerate until needed.

As a garnish, a few whole mushrooms may be placed on each piece of chicken breast.

CHICKEN A LA KING

1 chicken
1 cup mushrooms
4 tbsp butter
2 tbsp flour
1 cup milk

1 cup chicken stock
1 tbsp chopped pimento
1 tbsp W. sauce
1 tsp salt and pepper

Boil chicken with 3 cups water until tender and about 1½ cups of stock remain.

Slice mushrooms and fry in butter; then add flour, fry a little; gradually add hot chicken stock and milk, stir until the sauce thickens. Add salt, pepper, W. sauce, pimento and chopped chicken. Serve hot over vol-au-vents or over slices of fried bread.

Slices of pineapple can be placed over fried bread and the mixture poured over it. Garnish with chopped parsley.

Will serve six to eight people.

CHICKEN IN GARLIC

1 chicken
½ cup salad oil
½ tsp grated nutmeg
1 tsp salt
10 slices garlic

½ cup chopped celery
½ tsp freshly ground
 pepper
2 tbsp chopped parsley

Add oil to a casserol and toss chicken pieces in it, then add chopped celery, parsley, whole slices of garlic (peeled), salt, pepper and nutmeg, toss all this with the chicken, cover the casserol with the lid and place in a moderate oven for 2 hours, or until chicken is tender.

Serve hot with french fries and peas.

Will serve four to six people.

SAUTE OF CHICKEN

1 large chicken
3 large tomatoes
6 slices garlic
½ tsp pepper
1 dsp sugar
1 tsp salt
6 lamb kidneys

3 onions
½ tsp chilli powder
4 tbsp oil
2 tbsp chopped parsley
¼ cup sherry or port
 wine

Cut chicken into pieces and dredge with seasoned flour, and fry in hot oil or butter until golden brown.

Chop onions and tomatoes and garlic finely. Heat 2 tbsp oil in a pan and fry onions to golden brown; then add garlic and tomatoes, fry for a while, then add sliced kidneys and seasonings; add fried chicken and mix all; add 3 to 4 cups of water and cook until chicken is tender and 1 cup gravy remains. Just before serving, add port wine.

Serve chicken on a platter sprinkled with parsley and garnish with either hardboiled eggs or fried egg yolks.

Will serve four to six people.

CHICKEN WITH GREEN PEAS

1 large chicken	*12 small onions*
¼ kilo bacon	*½ kilo green peas*
2 large onions	*2 tbsp oil*
6 slices garlic	*2 large tomatoes*
2 tbsp chopped corian-	*3 green chillies*
der	*½ tsp chilli powder*
1 dsp salt, ¼ tsp pepper	*12 small potatoes*

Cut the chicken into pieces. Chop onions, garlic, chillies and tomatoes. Heat oil and fry onions until golden brown, add chopped bacon and fry; then add garlic, chillies and tomatoes, fry a little, add chicken pieces, add 4 cups of water and cook until chicken is tender.

Boil green peas and keep aside. Boil potatoes and peel, and fry them in some oil until brown, peel onions and fry them whole until golden, then add potatoes and onions to the chicken and simmer for 5 min, add chopped coriander, remove to a platter and cover with green peas.

Will serve four to six people.

CHICKEN WITH RAISINS

2 chickens	*½ cup raisins*
6 slices garlic	*2 capsicums cut into*
2 tbsp chopped green	*jullien strips*
chillies	*1 dsp salt and ¼ tsp*
1 cup pineapple juice	*pepper*

Cut chicken into pieces, dredge with flour (seasoned) and fry in oil until golden brown. Put all the pieces in the pan, drain off excess oil; then add chopped garlic, chillies and capsicums, saute for a few minutes and add salt, pepper and pineapple juice. Cover with lid and simmer until chicken is tender.

Wash and soak raisins in hot water until plump, then add to the chicken and cook for a few minutes more. Serve hot surrounded with slices of pineapple.

Will serve six to eight people.

CHICKEN ROYAL

2 large chickens
¼ tsp chilli powder
oil for frying

½ cup flour
salt, pepper

Cut chicken pieces, use the good pieces and make 2 cups chicken stock from the odd pieces. Dredge the chicken pieces with seasoned flour and fry in hot oil until golden; remove and keep aside.

Make chicken stock, chop pieces into a mush, add 4 cups cold water, 1 onion, a small piece of ginger, a stalk of celery, small piece of carrot and simmer until 2 cups stock remains. Strain and keep aside.

4 large onions
2 sliced carrots
2 tbsp lemon juice
1 cup thin cream
½ cup sherry

4 stalks of celery
¼ kilo sliced mushrooms
¼ kilo raw ham
2 egg yolks

Slice onions finely and add to the butter in which the chicken was fried, brown a little, add sliced carrots, celery, mushrooms; fry a little; add lemon juice and 2 cups chicken stock.

Lay the chicken pieces in a deep casserol, pour the vegetable mixture over it, fry pieces of ham and sprinkle over it. Cover the dish with lid and let the chicken cook until tender. The casserol can be placed in the oven or over a slow fire.

Just before serving, combine cream, egg yolks and remaining flour and add to the gravy; cook until thick, add sherry. Serve hot on a platter surrounded by small fried potatoes, or fried breadcubes.

Will serve eight to ten people.

CURRY FRIED CHICKEN

1 large chicken
½ cup flour
1 dsp salt, ¼ tsp pepper

2 cups chicken stock
¼ cup curry powder

Cut chicken into pieces, make stock from odd pieces.
Sift flour curry powder, salt and pepper. Roll the chicken pieces in it and fry to golden brown in oil or butter.
Remove from oil and in the same oil fry 2 chopped
onions until brown, then put in all the fried chicken
pieces in the pan, pour 1 cup stock over it and let it
simmer until chicken is tender; add more stock as needed.
When the chicken is cooked, remove pieces to a platter;
to the gravy add remaining mixture of flour and curry
powder and mix to a smooth sauce until it comes to a
boil. Pour over the chicken and serve with fried apple
slices.

Will serve four to six people.

CHICKEN TORERO

1 large chicken	*¼ cup flour*
1 tsp chilli powder	*2 tsp mustard powder*
1 tsp freshly ground	*2 tsp salt*
pepper	

Cut chicken into pieces. Mix flour, salt, pepper and
chilli powder and mustard powder.

Melt 4 tbsp butter in a baking dish. Roll chicken
pieces in the flour mixture and arrange them in the baking dish in which butter is melted, do not overlap them.
Melt another 2 tbsp of butter and pour over the chicken
pieces, bake in a moderate oven, until chicken is tender
and golden brown. Serve hot with french fries and boiled
vegetables.

Will serve four to six people.

CHICKEN IN RUM

1 chicken	*¼ cup cider vinegar*
½ cup brown sugar	*1 tsp salt, ¼ tsp pepper,*
2 tbsp lemon juice	*¼ cup rum*
4 tbsp butter	

Cut chicken into pieces and rub salt and freshly-
ground pepper. Melt butter and brown the chicken
pieces in it. Lower the heat, sprinkle sugar, lemon juice,

vinegar and rum, and cook over slow heat; if too dry add a little water, or put some water on the lid. Do not add too much water. Before serving, flambe with ¼ cup rum.
Will serve two to four people.

CHICKEN IN RUM WITH PINEAPPLE

2 chickens
½ cup butter
¼ cup rum
½ tsp tobasco
1 large tin pineapple

½ cup olive oil
6 slices garlic
2 dsp lemon juice, salt, pepper

Cut chicken into pieces, rub with salt and pepper. Melt butter and oil in a pan and fry the chicken pieces until brown; then add chopped garlic and fry for a while, lower the heat and add ¼ cup rum, tobasco, lemon juice and syrup from the pineapple tin. Cook on a very slow heat until chicken is tender. Before serving, add another ¼ cup of rum. Serve with glazed pineapple slices.

GLAZED PINEAPPLE SLICES: Sprinkle pineapple slices with some brown sugar and fry lightly in some butter.
Will serve six to eight people.

FRIED CHICKEN DIPPED IN SHERRY

1 large chicken
½ cup honey
2-3 eggs
1 cup sherry

breadcrumbs, flour, salt, pepper
oil for frying

Cut chicken into pieces and marinate in salt, pepper and sherry for 2 hours or overnight.

Drain chicken from the marinade, dredge in seasoned flour, then dip in beaten eggs, and then in breadcrumbs. Fry in oil on a very slow heat until brown; arrange all the pieces in a baking dish.

Mix honey with the drained marinade and pour over the chicken. Bake until the chicken is tender. Serve hot, sprinkled with parsley.
Will serve four to six people.

CHICKEN IN BEER

2 chickens
6 spring onions
6 bay leaves
1 bottle beer
1 tsp mixed herbs fresh
   or dry (basil, rose-
   mary, oregano)

1 dsp salt and ¼ tsp
   freshly ground pepper
½ cup butter
½ cup grated carrots
¼ tsp thyme
1 kilo red, ripe tomatoes

Cut chicken into pieces and apply salt and pepper. Fry in butter to a golden brown. Arrange all the pieces in a skillet, then sprinkle over it chopped onions, carrots, thyme, snipped bay leaves, herbs and skinned and finely chopped tomatoes. Pour beer over it all and simmer over low heat until chicken is tender.

Remove the chicken pieces to a platter. Blend 1 tbsp flour with ¼ cup water and add to the gravy, stir until thick, pour over the chicken and serve.

Will serve eight to ten people.

MASALA CHICKEN IN TOMATO GRAVY

1 chicken
6 slices garlic
6 peppercorns
4 cardamoms
4 large onions

8 red chillies
1 tsp cummin
1 piece cinnamon
1 kilo red ripe tomatoes
1 dsp sugar, 1 dsp salt

Cut chicken into pieces. Chop 3 onions finely and fry in ½ cup oil until golden, add chicken and fry for a while until lightly brown, keep aside. Wash tomatoes and chop. Add one chopped onion, ½ dsp salt and 1 cup water; boil all this and simmer until tomatoes are mushed, strain the juice through a sieve or use 2 cups tomato juice.

Grind chillies and all other masala to a paste with the vinegar, then fry this masala in ¼ cup oil, then add the tomato gravy, give one boil and then add all this to the fried chicken and cook on a slow fire until the chicken is cooked. Serve with fried potato chips, green peas and hardboiled eggs.

Will serve four to six people.

CHICKEN MASALA IN CURDS

1 large chicken	½ kilo curds
2 tsp chilli powder	2 tbsp poppy seeds
2 tsp cummin	1 piece ginger
2 onions	6 slices garlic
1 dsp salt	juice of 2 lemons
1 tbsp sugar	

Cut chicken into pieces.

Grind to a paste onions, ginger, garlic, cummin and poppyseeds, apply all this with the chilli powder, lemon juice and sugar and curd to the chicken pieces, and leave overnight in the refrigerator.

Next day, grease a baking dish well with oil, put chicken in it and bake in a moderate oven until chicken is cooked and some gravy remains.

Will serve four to six people.

MOGLAI CHICKEN

1 large chicken	8 Goa chillies
6 slices garlic	4 onions
4 cloves	1 piece ginger
1 piece cinnamon	4 cardamoms
½ tsp saffron to be soak-	1 tsp cummin
ed in 1 tsp of lemon	½ cup oil
juice	

Cut chicken into pieces, chop onions finely.

Grind all the masala to a fine paste.

Heat oil and fry the onions to golden brown, then add the ground masala and fry well over slow fire until the oil separates, then add chicken pieces, salt and fry for a while until chicken pieces are well coated with the masala. Add 6 cups hot water and let it simmer until the chicken is tender, add saffron soaked in lemon juice. Simmer for a few minutes and serve hot garnished with fried potato chips, green peas and hardboiled eggs.

Will serve four to six people.

MEATS

In India, mutton is the commonest of the meats eaten almost every day, but at present due to shortage of this meat, many people have taken to eating beef, veal and pork.

To make different dishes, right cuts of meat must be used.

The good and tender cuts must be used for roasting, grilling and frying. The tough cut must be used for mince, stews or in casserols.

Steaks, chops and escallops must be lightly beaten with a mallet to break the tissues, and soaked in a marinade for a few hours.

Meat cooked in a pressure cooker gets very tender in no time and retains its flavour. Meats must be cooked immediately on getting it home or leaving it in the refrigerator more so in the hot weather.

To boil meat, pour enough water to cover meat, bring to boil, boil for 5 minutes, then let it simmer until cooked.

Salted meats should be soaked in cold water for about two hours, a leg of raw ham or gam-

mon must be soaked overnight, then drain the
water off, add fresh water to the meat and bring
slowly to boil, then simmer till tender. If addi-
tional water is needed, add hot water; cold water
will bring down the temperature and toughen the
meat.

To grill meats, first heat the griller to red hot,
grease the grilling rack before placing the meat
on it, brush some oil or butter over the meat,
when half done season with salt and pepper,
place a dab of butter on it before serving.

Salt draws out the juice from the meats, so it
must be added when the meats are half cooked.
Do not use salt in your marinade.

Grilled meats are more digestible than fried
or roasted meats.

To pan fry, pour very little oil or butter in a
heavy fry pan, heat it well, then place the meat
in it and fry over high heat on both sides, then
lower the heat and cook to the required degree.

Do not put too many pieces of steaks or chops
at a time, fry few, remove, and fry the rest; when
all are fried, put them all together and cook.

To roast meats, heat the oven to "HOT", then
place the roast in a greased roasting pan, and
put it in the hot oven for about 20 minutes (this
seals the juices). After 20 minutes lower the oven
temperature to moderate or medium heat, then
cook the roast, basting with its own juice or with
the marinade.

If the roast is very lean, place some bacon
slices over it or rub some fat or butter.

To stew meat, cut into small serving pieces,
for casserol roll meat pieces in seasoned flour
and fry in hot oil.

Pork must always be very well cooked.

Pork if fresh must be pink in colour, fine grain, the fat must be white and the skin must be thin.

Leg of pork when roasted must be placed in a very hot oven for 20-30 minutes, then the heat lowered.

Pork chops must be marinated for quick cooking.

MUTTON KHURMA

1 kilo mutton	4 large onions
12 red chillies	1 tbsp dhania
12 slices garlic	1 piece ginger
1 piece cinnamon	6 cloves
6 cardamoms	6 peppercorns
1 tsp turmeric	4 tbsp ghee
1 dsp salt	¼ kilo curd
pinch of saffron	

Mix curd with saffron and keep it aside.

Grind chillies, garlic, ginger, dhania and turmeric to a paste and apply to the mutton pieces.

Pound the other spices to a fine powder.

Chop onions and fry in ghee until golden, then add the marinated mutton to it and fry until dry. Then add curd and saffron mixture to it, sprinkle the grounded spices and simmer over slow fire until the meat is cooked. Add 1 dsp of sugar, if desired.

Will serve six to eight people.

MUTTON KOFTA KHURMA

1 kilo mutton	1 tsp pepper
1 tsp turmeric	1 tsp dhanajeera
1 piece ginger	6 slices garlic
1 bunch coriander	6 green chillies
2 onions finely chopped	1 dsp salt

Mince the meat through a grinder twice, grind ginger and garlic, chop chillies and coriander, fry onions in a little oil until brown. To the meat apply ginger and garlic, then add to it all the dry ingredients, with chopped chillies, coriander and fried onions. Mix all this well into the meat, keep for an hour, then make into small koftas.

Khurma:

4 onions	1 tbsp sugar
6 slices garlic	1 piece ginger
3 tbsp poppy seeds	12 red chillies
2 dsp almonds or	1 tsp turmeric
cashew nuts	1 dsp salt
3 dsp dhania	1 kilo curds
½ cup oil	pinch of saffron

If the curd has too much water, drain it off, then beat with a beater until smooth; to this add saffron and sugar, mix well and leave it aside.

Chop onions finely and fry in oil until golden.

Grind to a paste ginger, garlic, chillies, dhania, poppy-seeds, almonds and turmeric. Add all this to the fried onions and fry well; then add to it the curd mixture, mix all well over slow fire, then put in the koftas and let it simmer until koftas are cooked and oil floats on top. Serve hot with chappaties or yellow rice.

Will serve six to eight people.

MUTTON WITH DRY APRICOTS

1 kilo mutton	¼ kilo dry apricots
2 large onions	6 green chillies
1 bunch coriander	6 slices garlic
1 piece ginger	1 tsp chilli powder
1 dsp lemon juice	1 dsp salt
6 peppercorns	1 piece cinnamon
4 cardamoms	4 cloves

Cut mutton into small pieces.

Grind to a paste ginger and garlic and apply to the mutton. Chop chillies and coriander. Wash and soak apricots in water, when soft remove the kernels, or if liked leave them whole. Chop onions and fry in ¼ cup oil until golden, then add the mutton pieces, and fry well until the water evaporates, then add 3 cups water and let the mutton simmer until cooked. When one cup gravy remains, add chillies and coriander and ground spices, cook for a while, then add apricots, lemon juice and 1 tsp sugar.

Will serve six to eight people.

CLASSIC VEAL STEW

1 kilo veal
4 tbsp butter
¼ kilo mushrooms
1 tbsp W. sauce
¼ kilo small onions
  (boiled)
½ kilo green peas
  (boiled)
4 tbsp flour

½ dsp salt
½ tsp pepper
½ cup chopped onions
2 cups chicken or veal
  stock
6 slices chopped bacon
¼ kilo baby carrots
  (boiled)
1 cup cream

Cut veal into cubes, roll in flour seasoned with salt and pepper.

Melt butter and fry the veal cubes in it until brown, remove from the pan, add onions to the butter and fry brown, then add sliced mushrooms and bacon, fry until brown, then stir in the seasoned flour which has remained, blend in stock and stir until thick, then add veal cubes and simmer on slow fire until veal is tender. Just before serving add W. sauce and cream. Serve it on a platter surrounded by boiled carrots, onions and peas.

¼ cup sherry may be added.
Will serve four to six people.

VEAL CUTLETS VIENNA

1 kilo thin veal cutlets
  (veal sliced thin and
  pounded between two
  pieces of cloth)
4 tbsp butter
1 cup cream

½ tsp pepper
1 cup stock (veal or
  chicken)
2 tbsp flour
¼ cup red or white wine
1 dsp salt

Season cutlets with salt and pepper and brown in butter on both sides until cooked, remove to a serving dish. In the same pan add flour, salt and one cup starch and stir until it boils and thickens then add cream and wine, stir and pour over cutlets, serve hot. Sherry or gin may be added instead of wine.

Will serve four to six people.

MUTTON GOULASH

1 kilo mutton
6 slices chopped garlic
2 tbsp brown sugar
1 tsp caraway seeds
salt and ½ tsp pepper

1 cup tomato ketchup
1 cup chopped onions
1 tsp chilli powder
1 tsp dill seeds
1 dsp salt

Cut mutton into cubes, mix all the above ingredients to it, add 1 cup water and simmer until the mutton is cooked, add 2 tsp butter before serving. Serve hot on a bed of mashed potatoes, or with dumplings.

Dumplings:

2 cups flour
1 tsp salt
½ cup milk

2 large eggs
1 tbsp melted butter
2 tsp baking powder

Sift flour, salt and baking powder three times, beat eggs lightly, add milk, stir into the flour, beating well; the batter should be smooth and thick. (It can be beaten in an electric mixer).

In a large pan, boil 8 cups of water with 1 dsp of salt, drop 1 rounded tsp of batter into the boiling water until all the dumplings are made. Close the pan and remove the lid after about 20-30 minutes; if the dumplings are floating on top, they are ready, remove them with slotted spoon on to a hot platter, pour some melted butter over it and serve. (Chopped parsley, caraway seeds, cheese or paprika can be added as variations.)
Will serve six to eight people.

VEAL MILANO

8 veal or beef chops well trimmed, about 1″ thick, to be marinated in 2 tsp salad oil, 2 tbsp lemon juice, and pepper overnight in the refrigerator.

1 cup breadcrumbs
½ tsp paprika
Mix all the four ingred-
   ients together

3 eggs beaten slightly
1 cup grated cheese
1 tsp salt
flour

Drain the chops from the marinade, roll in flour seasoned with salt and pepper, dip in eggs and then in the
breadcrumbs mixture, put in the refrigerator for half an
hour.

Sauce:

½ cup salad oil
2 cups chopped tomatoes
1 tbsp sugar
1 tsp oregano or basil if
   available

12 slices garlic
1 cup tomato ketchup
dash of monosodium
   glutamate
salt and pepper

Heat oil in a pan and fry the chopped garlic until golden, add chopped tomatoes and tomato ketchup with
all the seasonings, simmer for 15 minutes.

Fry chops in hot oil over a slow fire until nearly cooked and brown on both sides. Arrange them all in a
shallow casserol. Pour the sauce over and bake until
chops are tender. Serve hot.

Will serve four to six people.

VEAL PUERTO RICO

1 kilo boneless veal
6 slices garlic
½ cup tomato ketchup
½ tsp tobasco
½ cup pimento
3 onions

4 tbsp butter
1 tbsp W. sauce
1 cup chopped cashew
   nuts
1 tbsp flour, salt and
   pepper

Cut veal into cubes, mince garlic, apply to the veal
with pepper. Melt butter and fry finely chopped onions
until golden brown, remove from the butter and fry veal
cubes in the same butter until brown, mix tomato ketchup
with one cup water and pour over the fried cubes with
salt, add onions and let it simmer until the meat is tender,
then add tobasco, nuts and flour mixed in a little cold
water and W. sauce. Serve hot garnished with sliced
pimento. Capsicum can be used.

Will serve four to six people.

VEAL HAPSBURG

1 kilo veal	¼ cup salad oil
½ tsp paprika or chilli powder	4 tbsp butter
	6 slices garlic
¼ cup chopped onions	½ cup beef stock
2 tbsp flour	1 tbsp lemon juice
½ cup sour cream	1 dsp salt
½ cup dry white wine	½ tsp pepper

Wash veal, dry with a cloth and cut into cutlets ¼"
thick, season with salt and pepper. Heat oil and fry the
cutlets on slow fire until tender, keep hot on a platter.
To the hot oil add butter, onions and minced garlic.
Saute until soft, lower the heat and add flour, paprika,
and cook over low heat until thick. Add cream and
lemon juice, salt and pepper, stir in beef stock and wine,
pour the sauce over the fried veal cutlets.

Will serve four to six people.

BEEF BURGERS IN MUSHROOM SAUCE

1 kilo boneless beef	2 tbsp chopped parsley
¼ cup mayonnaise	½ cup breadcrumbs
1 tsp. made mustard	6 slices cheese (processed)
2 eggs	
1 tin cream of mushroom soup	¼ cup milk
oil for frying	1 dsp salt
2 tbsp onions	½ tsp pepper

Mince beef add onions, mayonnaise, salt, pepper, parsley, mustard; mix all this together, then form into 6
round patties, beat eggs slightly, dip patties in egg and
then in breadcrumbs, brown lightly in oil, and place in
a glass baking dish, cut each slice of cheese in two and
lay over the patties in a cross. Combine soup and milk,
pour over the patties and bake in a moderate oven for
15 min. Serve hot.

Any other soup can be used, such as celery, tomato
or chicken.

Will serve six to eight people.

MEATBALLS AND BAKED BEANS CASSEROL

½ kilo ground beef	½ kilo ground pork
¼ cup breadcrumbs	2 tbsp chopped parsley
2 tbsp chopped celery	2 tbsp grated cheese
6 slices garlic	¼ cup milk, oil
2 eggs	½ dsp salt
2 tbsp finely chopped onion	½ tsp pepper

MEATBALLS: Combine all the above ingredients and mix well, shape into small balls and brown in oil, remove them to a casserol.

Sauce:

1 tin baked beans	2 tbsp butter
6 slices garlic	½ kilo chopped tomatoes
½ tsp chilli powder	1 cup tomato ketchup
½ cup finely chopped onions	salt and pepper

Melt butter and fry chopped onions and garlic until golden brown, add chilli powder, chopped tomatoes, beans, tomato ketchup, salt and pepper, bring all this to a boil and pour over the meatballs.

Bake for 15 min. in a moderate oven.

If liked, a few chopped green chillies may be added to the sauce.

Will serve eight to ten people.

MEATBALLS IN BEAN SAUCE

½ kilo minced beef	2 slices bread
¼ kilo minced pork	1 tbsp chilli sauce
¼ cup milk	1 tbsp soya sauce
2 tbsp brown sugar	2 eggs
2 tbsp chopped onion	2 tins baked beans
¼ kilo bacon	½ tsp mustard powder
3 tbsp golden syrup	½ cup tomato ketchup
2 onions	½ dsp salt
¼ cup rum	½ tsp pepper
½ kilo minced raw ham	

Soak bread in hot milk, mash it up and mix with beef, ham, pork, salt, chilli sauce, brown sugar, soya sauce, onion and eggs. Mix all well and form into balls and refrigerate.

In a pan, fry chopped bacon until crisp, then add baked beans, golden syrup, mustard, 2 chopped onions, tomato ketchup, salt, pepper and one cup water, bring to boil, lower the heat and place the meatballs in it, simmer until the balls are cooked. Add rum before serving.

Will serve eight to ten people.

BROILED STEAK

6 beef steaks, 1" thick, marinate in the following marinade and to be kept in the refrigerator overnight.

Marinade:

½ cup olive oil or salad oil
1 tbsp prepared mustard

2 tbsp lemon juice
1 tsp freshly ground pepper, salt

Turn the steaks in the marinade once or twice in the day.

Sprinkle salt over the marinated steak just before broiling. Broil the steaks on both sides until done to your liking. Serve immediately with french fries and onion rings, fried in batter, or just boiled.

Will serve six people.

BEEF STEW

1 kilo boneless beef
½ cup salad oil
¼ kilo mushrooms
3 beef cubes
2 dsp W. sauce
¼ kilo small onions
¼ kilo small potatoes
½ cup flour, seasoned with ½ tsp salt
¼ tsp pepper

2 tbsp chopped parsley
3 onions minced
6 slices garlic minced
3 cups hot water
½ cup tomato sauce
¼ kilo sliced carrots
¼ kilo green peas
1 tsp salt
½ tsp pepper

Cut beef into cubes, dredge with seasoned flour and fry in hot salad oil until brown; remove from pan, add onions and garlic and fry, then add the remaining seasoned flour, stir in 3 cups hot beef bouillon, simmer until the beef is nearly tender, then add potatoes, carrots, onions, mushrooms and peas; cook until the beef and vegetables are tender; add tomato ketchup and W. sauce. Serve hot sprinkled with parsley.

Will serve eight to ten people.

BEEF STEW ITALIAN

1 kilo boneless beef	3 large onions
6 slices garlic	½ cup tomato puree
1 kilo tomatoes, small	½ cup chopped parsley
1 tsp mixed herbs	½ tsp chilli powder
½ cup chopped parsley	½ cup grated cheese
¼ kilo macaroni	(parmisan, if available)
1 cup salad oil	

Cut beef into cubes; fry in salad oil until brown, season with salt and pepper; remove and add quartered onions and sliced garlic, fry a little, then add tomatoes (dipped in hot water and skinned and left whole), tomato puree, herbs (Oregano, thyme, basil or rosemary), and chilli powder, then add 1 beef cube dissolved in 1 cup hot water. Simmer until beef is cooked.

Boil macaroni in salt water, drain, add cheese, mix well and serve, round the beef stew sprinkled with chopped parsley.

Will serve six to eight people.

CARBONADE OF BEEF

12 slices of round rump steak	6 onions
6 slices garlic	½ tsp powdered thyme
1 tsp pepper	1 cup beef stock
1 dsp prepared mustard	½ bottle beer
4 tbsp butter	1 tbsp cornflour
	1 dsp salt

Slice onions finely and fry in butter until golden brown.

Dip the beef slices in some flour and brown gently on both sides in the same butter after removing the onions. Remove the steaks to a casserol and fry garlic in the same butter, add a little more butter if necessary, add to it thyme, salt, mustard, stock and beer, pour all this over the fried beef slices, sprinkle fried onions over it, close the lid and bake in a moderate oven until the beef is done; just before serving, heat the dish and add cornflour mixed in a little cold water.

Will serve six people.

AFRICAN BOBOTEE

1 kilo raw minced beef or mutton	3 tbsp apricot jam
1 tbsp curry powder	4 tbsp butter
3 onions	2 tbsp lemon juice
2 tbsp raisins	2 thick slices of bread
1 dsp salt and ½ tsp pepper	4 tbsp almond or cashew
	½ cup beef stock

Sauce:

4 cups milk	2 tbsp cornflour
3 eggs	salt and pepper

Mix cornflour in a little cold milk, beat the eggs lightly and add to the milk with the cornflour and salt, pepper; stir over low heat until the mixture thickens; do not boil, cool.

Slice the onions finely and fry in butter until golden. Soak bread in water and squeeze it dry, add to the fried onions and mash, add the minced meat and all the seasonings, fry until the meat browns, then add stock and lemon juice, cook for 10 minutes. Add fried raisins, nuts and apricot jam, turn all this in a well buttered baking dish, and smooth the top, cover this with the milk mixture, sprinkle with some breadcrumbs, and bake in a hot oven until the top is brown. Serve hot with a cucumber salad. This dish can be served cold.

Will serve eight to ten people.

Cucumber Salad:

¼ *kilo very thinly sliced*   *pinch chilli powder*
  cucumber   *1 dsp sugar*
1 cup well drained curds   *salt, pepper*
2 dsp vinegar

Slice the cucumbers, apply 1 dsp of salt and leave for 15 min., then wash and drain all the liquid. Mix curds with all the seasonings and pour over the cucumber; chill and serve.

ROULAD OF BEEF

12 slices round steak   *1 capsicum chopped*
3 tbsp chopped onions   *2 cups beef stock*
1 tsp prepared mustard   *1 dsp salt*
1 cup red wine   *½ tsp pepper*
12 small gherkins

Pound the steak thin between two pieces of cloth, lay on each piece of steak a gherkin, a little chopped onion, salt, pepper and a little mustard. Roll the steak and put toothpicks in each, dip each roll in flour and fry in butter until brown. Put all the fried rolls in a pan, pour beef stock and wine over it and simmer until the rolls are cooked. If the gravy is thin, add a little cornflour mixed in a little cold water.
Will serve six people.

MIXED MEAT LOAF

½ *kilo minced beef*   ½ *kilo minced veal*
½ *kilo minced pork*   *1 cup breadcrumbs*
3 eggs   *2 minced onions*
1 dsp curry powder   ½ *cup milk*
1 dsp salt   *1 tsp pepper*

Mix thoroughly all the above ingredients together, and form into a loaf, place on a well-buttered baking dish and bake in a moderate oven until well done and brown, baste with butter once or twice. Serve sliced hot or cold with a salad.

To make a barbecued loaf, make it the same way as above, but after 30 minutes of baking, pour the under-mentioned sauce, half first and the rest later, and bake in all for about 2 hours or until nicely brown.

Serve hot with french fries and boiled vegetables. It makes a nice buffet dish or a main dish. Serve in the same dish.

Will serve twelve to fifteen people.

Barbecued Sauce:

1 cup tomato ketchup	¼ cup W. sauce
½ cup water	2 dsp chilli sauce
¾ cup brown sugar	2 dsp lemon juice
1 dsp curry powder	½ tsp pepper, salt
4 tbsp butter	

Mix all the above ingredients in a bowl, put them in hot water until butter melts. Pour half to half as directed above.

Will serve eight to ten people.

VEAL CONTINENTAL

1 kilo boneless veal	½ tsp pepper
¼ kilo slices processed cheese	2 tbsp grated onion
2 cups chicken stock	2 tbsp butter
1 large tin mushrooms	4 tbsp finely chopped onions
6 slices garlic	a few drops of tobasco
2 tbsp cornflour	½ cup any dry wine or ¼ cup brandy
½ dsp salt	few sliced olives
¼ kilo raw ham or cooked (sliced)	

Wash the whole piece of veal and wipe it dry, then cut into ¼" thick slices, put between two layers of cloth and pound it thin. Make as many slices as you can; each slice should be 5 x 5".

On each slice of veal, put a slice of ham and then a slice of cheese, sprinkle a little salt and pepper and onion over it, and make into a roll, pierce toothpicks to keep the rolls in shape. Put all these rolls into a wide pan;

add two cups of stock, and let it simmer on a slow fire until the rolls are tender. Remove them from the gravy, discard the toothpicks and place the rolls in a serving dish or a covered casserol.

Melt butter and fry chopped onions and garlic to a golden brown, then fry the sliced mushrooms in it, add seasonings and the gravy from the rolls. Boil a little if the gravy is too thin. Mix cornflour with a little cold water and add to the boiling gravy. When thick remove from fire, add wine or brandy. Pour the whole thing over the rolls and serve hot.

This dish can be prepared and kept; before serving, heat it in the oven, and pour wine or brandy just before serving.

Will serve twelve people.

GAMMON WITH APRICOT SAUCE

2 kg piece of gammon, to be soaked in water overnight. Next day wash it, scrub it and lay in a greased pan, add 1 cup water and bake in a moderate oven until it is tender. Then slice it and arrange on a flat dish or platter, and pour the sauce over it.

Apricot Sauce:

1 tin apricots	*½ cup apricot jam*
2 tbsp butter	*1 tbsp grated orange rind*
2 tbsp flour	*¼ tsp salt*
2 tbsp lemon juice	*¼ tsp pepper*
1 beef or chicken cube	*½ tsp grated nutmeg*
1 tsp mustard powder	*6 cloves*

Drain the apricots and puree them. Strain the puree. Melt the butter, add flour and fry for a while, then add the apricot puree with the rest of the ingredients. Stir until thick; if too thick, add some of the apricot syrup. Cook over low heat, stirring all the time, for about ten minutes. It must be a good sauce-like consistency. Strain the sauce through a medium sieve. Heat the sauce before serving, and pour over the gammon slices. A little brandy may be added.

Serve with parsley potatoes and boiled vegetables.

Will serve six to eight people.

GAMMON WITH PEACHES

3 kg leg of gammon to be soaked in water overnight.

1 tin of peaches (large)	*½ cup peach or apricot*
½ cup maraschino	*jam*
cherries	*4 cloves*
½ cup honey	*¼ cup brown sugar*
1 tsp mustard powder	*¼ cup brandy*
½ tsp cayenne pepper	

Scrub the leg of gammon and boil in water, to which has been added juice of 2 lemons, 2 tbsp brown sugar and 4 cloves. When thoroughly cooked, remove from water and skin it. Place the leg in a baking dish, scour the top into diamonds, and pierce a clove into each joint. Then pour some glaze over it and bake in a moderate oven, keep pouring the glaze until all the glaze is over, and the top is well-glazed. Serve the whole leg on a platter surrounded by peaches and maraschino cherries. (Tinned cherries can be used).

The gravy in the pan must be served separately in a sauce-boat. 2 tbsp brandy can be added to it, if desired.

Will serve twelve to fifteen people.

Glaze:

Drain syrup from the peaches, mix with honey, mustard, cayenne, jam and brandy. Heat and use as glaze.

PORK CHOPS IN ORANGE JUICE

8 pork chops	*1 dsp. salt*
2 cups orange juice	*½ tsp freshly ground*
2 tbsp brown sugar	*pepper*
1 tsp cinnamon powder	*few orange segments,*
1 tbsp cornflour	*peeled*

Trim pork chops, and fry in a skillet until golden brown on both sides. Arrange them all flat and add orange juice, sugar, salt and pepper and simmer over low heat until chops are cooked. Remove them on a platter.

Mix cornflour with a little water and add to the sauce with cinnamon, stir until thick. Add orange segments and pour over the chops. Serve hot.

Brandy may be added to the sauce, if desired.
Will serve four to eight people.

INDONESIAN PORK

1 kg pork
¼ cup salad oil
¼ cup lemon juice
¼ cup soya sauce
2 tbsp curry powder
1 blade chopped lemon
grass

1 dsp chilli powder
6 slices garlic
4 onions, finely chopped
4 green chillies, finely
chopped
¼ cup honey
½ dsp salt

Wash the pork and cut into pieces, mix lemon juice, soya sauce, curry powder, chopped lemon grass, chilli powder, chopped garlic and chillies and add to the pork and marinate for an hour.

Heat oil and fry onions until golden, add pork to it and honey. Cook over low heat until the pork is tender. If required, add a little water.

The marinated pork can be kept in the refrigerator overnight.
Will serve six people.

ROAST PORK WITH RAISIN SAUCE

2½ kg leg of pork
12 slices garlic
1 tsp roasted cummin
seeds

1 tsp oregano (if avail-
able)
1 dsp salt

Wash the leg of pork, chop garlic. Rub the pork with garlic, cummin seeds, oregano and salt. Put in a roasting pan and bake in a moderate oven until the pork is well cooked, remove the skin (whilst hot). Put on a platter and pour sauce over it.

For easy serving, the pork can be sliced and arranged on a flat dish and hot sauce poured over it just before serving.

Raisin Sauce:

½ bottle tomato ketchup   ½ tsp pepper
1 cup water   1 cup raisins
¼ cup flour   ½ cup sliced olives
1 tsp chilli powder   ½ tsp salt

After removing the pork from the baking dish, drain off most of the pork fat from the top of the dripping. Heat the dripping in a pan, add flour and stir until smooth. Then add water, ketchup and seasonings. Stir until smooth, boil for 2 min. then strain and add cleaned and washed raisins and olives. Cook for another 2 min. and pour over the pork.

Will serve ten to twelve people.

PORK MEXICAN

2½ kg leg of pork   ½ tsp freshly ground
1 dsp salt   pepper
½ cup rum

Rub pork with salt, pepper and rum, and leave it in the refrigerator overnight. Next day, put the leg in a greased baking dish and roast in a moderate oven until tender. Slice and serve with the following sauce.

Sauce:

½ cup olive oil   1 tsp salt
2 tbsp lemon juice   3 red pimentoes
¼ cup cider vinegar   ½ tsp chilli powder
6 peppercorns   6 slices garlic

Blend all this in a blender, and serve with the pork.
Will serve ten to twelve people.

PORK CHOPS IN PINEAPPLE SAUCE

8 pork chops	¼ cup cider vinegar
1 large tin pineapple	¼ cup tomato ketchup
1 tbsp oil	2 tbsp soya sauce
3 onions, finely chopped	1 dsp curry powder
8 slices garlic, chopped	½ tsp pepper
2 tbsp corn flour	½ cup brown sugar

Trim the chops, wash them and dry them on a clean cloth. Heat one tbsp oil in a pan and fry 4 chops at a time to a golden brown. Remove from the pan to a baking dish, laying them all flat.

Add onions and garlic in the same pan, and fry until a little brown, drain the pineapple juice from the can and mix all other ingredients into it and pour over the fried onions, give it a boil, stirring constantly, remove and pour over the chops. Cover the dish and bake in a moderate oven until the chops are tender. Mix cornflour in a little cold water and add to the chops, stir well, leave in the oven for another 10 minutes, and serve with sliced pineapple.

Will serve four to eight people.

DEVILLED PORK CHOPS

8 pork chops	1 tsp mustard powder
½ cup chopped onions	1 dsp salt, ½ tsp pepper
1 dsp curry powder	freshly ground
2 tbsp lemon juice	1 tsp chilli sauce
2 tbsp Worcester sauce	2 tbsp golden syrup

Trim chops and wash and dry them on a clean cloth.

Mix all other ingredients together, and marinate the chops in it for an hour. Heat 2 tbsp oil in a skillet, drain the chops from the marinade, and fry them golden brown (few at a time.) Place all the chops in a baking pan and pour the marinade, mixed with one cup water, over the chops. Close the pan and simmer on a slow fire, until the chops are done. Serve with french fries and boiled peas.

This can be prepared in a pressure cooker by adding 1 cup extra water.

Will serve four to eight people.

SPICED TONGUE

2 ox tongues	12 peppercorns
4 sour limes	1 tbsp saltpeter
2 heaped tbsp brown	1½ cup salt
sugar	2 tbsp vinegar

Wash tongues and marinate in all the above ingredients, cut the sour limes into halves and squeeze the juice over the tongues and rub the tongues with the rind. Leave the squeezed lemon halves in the marinade. Keep in a glass dish or a stainless steel pan and keep in refrigerator for at least 4-6 days, turning every day in the marinade.

After four days remove the lemon rind, add water to cover the tongues and boil until the tongues are tender. Cool a little, remove from the stock and peel the skin off the tongue.

Chill and cut into thin slices and serve cold. It can also be served in the following Apricot Sauce.

Apricot Sauce:

¼ kilo dry apricots	½ tsp salt
½ cup brown sugar	⅓ cup vinegar
12 peppercorns	2 x 1 inch pieces cinna-
8 cardamoms	mon
2 tbsp rum	6 cloves

Soak apricots in cold water for about ½ hour, drain off the water, add 2 cups water again and soak overnight.

Next day remove the kernels from the apricots, add all the above ingredients, and bring to a boil. Simmer until apricots are tender, then remove from fire and cool.

Then puree it in a liquidizer, strain through a fine sieve and leave until serving time.

Heat sauce and add 2 tbsp butter and stir until butter melts, add a little cocheanel for colour. Add 2 tbsp rum and pour over the sliced tongue.

This sauce will be enough for 1 sliced tongue or a little more. Serves about 20 people for buffet.

VEGETABLES

Vegetables are a must on every menu; they may be used as an accompaniment to a main dish, or as a dish in itself.

In India we have more variety of vegetable dishes than anywhere else in the world. Of course, we have a lot of people who are complete vegetarians, and so we have invented a lot of vegetarian dishes.

Vegetables are best when fresh and crisp.

Vegetables must not be overcooked, they lose their flavour and colour, and also the vitamins and mineral contents, and thus have their nutritional value reduced.

Vegetables, if possible, must be soaked for a while in water to which a pinch of permanganate of potash has been added, then wash in fresh water.

Vegetables that are cooked with the skin must be scrubbed well; when they are to be peeled, they must be very thinly pared with a vegetable parer or a very sharp knife.

Vegetables cooked in a pressure cooker retain more of their nutritional value, but must not be overcooked.

Most vegetables must be cooked in covered pans.

Vegetables taste best when gently sauted in small amount of butter, the pan then closed, and the vegetables allowed to cook in their own juice.

For Chinese cooking, vegetables should be cut into jullien strips fried quickly in very little oil over very high heat in a thick pan, stirred frequently and removed while still crisp.

Undercooked vegetables are easy to digest.

Salt must be added to the vegetables just after they are cooked, otherwise they get too soft.

When boiling vegetables, add a few drops of lemon juice; by doing this, the colour is retained (1 tsp lemon juice to 2 cups of water).

Frozen vegetables must be thawed completely before cooking, and cooked immediately on thawing, they may be added straight to the cooked meat or any casserols.

When boiling vegetables, the water should be brought to boil, the heat then lowered, and the vegetables simmered gently until cooked.

Vegetables should not be soaked after they are peeled, only peeled potatoes are to be soaked, as they get discoloured.

Root vegetables may be soaked in salted cold water, with a little vinegar, to draw out any insects.

POTATOES

Potatoes are the best liked vegetable, by the young and the old. In some form or other, the potato must be on the daily menu of most families. It is available all the year round and makes dishes instantly when guests arrive unexpectedly.

Choose medium and equal-size potatoes for boiling and roasting; for baked potatoes use large kidney potatoes.

To boil potatoes, bring the water to boil first, add salt and potatoes and boil steadily until tender.

When making mashed potatoes, press the potatoes through a masher, as soon as it is done, always add hot milk to the mashed potatoes, never cold milk, as it makes the potatoes sticky.

To roast potatoes, peel them, cover with cold water and bring to a boil, then drain them, dip in seasoned flour and place round the roast, basting frequently with the gravy, turn once during cooking to brown evenly. If they are to be served separately, fry them in deep hot oil.

Small potatoes can be boiled, peeled and tossed in butter until lightly browned. Serve sprinkled with chopped parsley, chives or bacon.

For baked potatoes, scrub them whilst washing, then wipe them dry with a towel, rub a little oil all over, and put in a slow oven for about 1-1½ hours. Choose even-sized potatoes. Turn the potatoes once or twice whilst baking, keep them apart from one another. When soft, make a deep cross with a sharp knife on top of each potato, hold the potato with a cloth, then gently squeeze with both hands so that the potato comes up through the opening. Serve with sour cream and chives dressing.

TO FRY POTATOES

1 POTATO CHIPS: Peel and cut potatoes into chips, soak in cold water for about an hour. Heat oil in a deep frier, fry the chips until half-fried then remove on absorbent paper and leave until cold, while frying the remain-

ing chips.   Just before serving, heat the oil until it smokes;
then add the half-fried chips and fry until golden; drain
on paper, sprinkle with salt, pepper and cayenne pepper
and serve hot.   Do not add too many chips to the oil.

2 *POTATO CHIPS*:   Peel and cut potatoes into chips,
add water and salt just to cover, give it one or two boils
and remove, drain from the water, cool, then fry in very
hot deep oil until golden and crisp.

3 *MASHED POTATOES*:

4 *large potatoes (soft*	$\frac{1}{2}$ *tsp freshly ground*
variety)	*pepper*
2 *dsp butter*	1 *dsp salt*
$\frac{3}{4}$ *cup hot milk*	$\frac{1}{4}$ *tsp nutmeg*

Peel potatoes and boil them until tender, keep on low
heat until all the water dries up, mash the potatoes with
a masher or put through a ricer, beat until smooth, adding hot milk and butter, when light and fluffy add seasoning and serve hot.

DUCHESS POTATOES

Make mash potatoes as above without milk, add 1 egg
instead and beat well, put in a pastry bag and pipe rosette
on a greased baking sheet, bake until golden.   Serve
around meat dishes.

POTATO CROQUETTES

Make mash potatoes as for duchess potatoes, form into
small croquettes, dip in seasoned flour, then in beaten
egg and roll them in fine breadcrumbs, fry in deep hot
oil, drain on paper before serving.
For variation, you can add 2 tbsp cheese, 2 tbsp
chopped ham or 2 tbsp crisply fried bacon or chopped
parsley to the potatoes.
If preferred hot, add some chopped chillies, coriander
and chilli powder.

COTTAGE CHEESE

2 *lit. milk* $\frac{1}{2}$ *cup curd*

Boil milk, cool to lukewarm. Beat curd in a pan and add slightly warm milk to it gradually, mixing well.

Put it in a warm place overnight. Next morning when it is set, put the whole lot in a fine muslin cloth, put over a strainer, and drain off all the water; when firm, beat in ½ cup cream and salt and mix well.

Makes 2 cups.

COTTAGE CHEESE MOULD

Cottage cheese made from 1 litre milk.

2 eggs	½ cup breadcrumbs
¾ cup milk	1 tbsp salad oil
1 cup finely chopped celery	1 tbsp minced spring onions
1 tsp salt	¼ tsp pepper
½ cup chopped walnuts	1 dsp castor sugar
1 tbsp W. sauce	

Beat eggs, add milk and seasonings; mix well then add breadcrumbs, celery, onions and walnuts. Mix well, and pour in a well greased 8" square mould, put in a pan of hot water and bake in a moderate oven until the mould is firm. Unmould and serve with mushroom sauce.

Mushroom Sauce:

1 pkt or tin of mush-room soup	2 cups water
1 cup sliced mushrooms	2 tbsp butter, salt, ¼ tsp pepper

Fry mushrooms in butter, add hot water to the soup and add to the mushrooms and boil until thick. Pour over the mould and serve.

Will serve six to eight people.

MACARONI CHEESE LOAF

3 cups grated processed cheese	2 tbsp finely minced spring onion
½ tsp mustard powder	Few drops tobasco
½ cup thick mayonnaise	

Line a loaf pan with foil on all sides and bottom. **Mix** all the above ingredients together and apply the mixture all round and the bottom of the loaf pan, about ¼″ thick. Chill the pan.

Filling:

3 cups cooked macaroni	½ cup chopped celery
½ cup chopped capsicum	2 tbsp chopped onion
½ cup chopped gherkin	1 cup grated cheese
½ cup mayonnaise	1 tsp salt, ½ tsp pepper

Boil the macaroni, drain and add all the above ingredients to the hot macaroni, mix well and cool the **mix**ture. Pack all this firmly in the cheese lined loaf **pan.** Cover with a piece of foil and chill the mould in **the** refrigerator overnight.

Before serving, unmould the loaf on a platter, remove the foil carefully and garnish with slices of tomatoes **and** hardboiled eggs.

Will serve twelve to fourteen people.

BRUSSELS SPROUTS IN CREAM

1 kilo Brussels sprout	¼ kilo bacon
6 slices bread	4 tbsp cider vinegar
1 cup cream	1 tsp salt, ¼ tsp pepper

Boil sprouts and drain. Chop bacon and fry crisp in its own fat, remove the bacon from the fat and fry bread cubes in it, if needed add a little butter, fry them crisp and golden, add hot brussels sprout, bacon and seasonings, add cream, toss well and serve hot. Do not boil after adding cream.

Will serve six to eight people.

SWEET AND SOUR BAKED BEANS

2 tins baked beans
¼ cup french dressing
1 cup finely chopped
  celery
¼ cup chopped gherkin
1 tsp mustard powder
2 tbsp chilli sauce

½ cup tomato ketchup
½ cup sliced spring
  onions
2 tbsp brown sugar
½ tsp salt
½ tsp pepper

Combine all the above ingredients together and mix well, chill, serve cold garnished with wedges of tomatoes and sprinkled with parsley.
Will serve six to eight people.

BAKED BEANS WITH PINEAPPLE

2 tins baked beans
¼ cup chilli sauce
2 tsp instant coffee
1 large tin pineapple
  slices

½ cup tomato ketchup
1 tbsp brown sugar
¼ cup hot water
½ tsp salt, ½ tsp pepper
brown sugar

Mix baked beans, ketchup, salt, pepper, chilli sauce brown sugar and coffee mixed in ¼ cup hot water. Put all this in a greased baking dish. Half an hour before serving lay slices of pineapple over the beans, sprinkle with some brown sugar and bake until the top browns.
  2 tbsp of rum may be added to the beans, if liked.
Will serve six to eight people.

SPINACH SOUFFLE

3 cups fresh boiled
  spinach
½ cup grated cheese
1 cup milk
½ cup breadcrumbs
1 tsp grated nutmeg

½ cup chopped onions
2 tbsp butter
4 eggs
1 dsp salt, ½ tsp pepper
1 tbsp W. sauce

Fry onions in butter until golden, add boiled spinach,
salt, pepper and nutmeg, mix well, then slightly beat eggs
and add milk; add this to the spinach, stir in cheese,
breadcrumbs and W. sauce.

Butter well a souffle dish and pour the spinach mixture
in it, put the dish in a pan of hot water and bake in a
moderate oven for about 30 min. or until it sets.

Will serve six to eight people.

SAVOURY VEGETABLE PIE

1 x 9" pie shell unbaked	*3 tomatoes*
3 capsicums	*3 onions*
1 cup milk	*½ cup cream*
3 eggs	*1 tsp salt, ½ tsp pepper*

Slice tomatoes, capsicum and onions. Heat ¼ cup
salad oil in a pan and fry onions and capsicum until
soft; drain the liquid from the tomato slices and add to
the onion capsicum mixture; add salt and pepper and
cook for 5 minutes, then cool. Pour the vegetable mixture
in the prepared pie shell.

Beat eggs slightly with milk and cream and seasonings.
Pour over the vegetable mixture and bake in a moderate
oven for about 45 min. or until pie is set. Garnish with
some capsicum rings before serving.

Serve hot or cold.

Pie Shell:

2 cups flour	*1 egg*
½ cup butter	*½ tsp salt*

Sift flour with salt, rub in butter until it is like fine
crumbs add egg and form into a dough; if required, add
some water. Line the dough in a buttered pie dish.

Will serve six to eight people.

CAULIFLOWER STUFFED PUREES

Purees:

2 cups whole wheat flour	1 dsp salt
½ tsp chilli powder	½ tsp turmeric
1 tsp cummin pounded	1 dsp ghee

Make a pliable dough with the above ingredients, using as much water as needed. Leave the dough aside for an hour or two.

Stuffing:

2 cups finely chopped cauliflower	½ tsp chilli powder
	6 green chillies
½ cup grated coconut	1 dsp sugar
2 tbsp chopped coriander	1 tsp salt
½ cup roasted chopped cashew nuts	1 tbsp oil
	juice of 2 lemons

Heat oil, fry lightly chopped chillies, then add chilli powder, coconut, sugar, salt and cauliflower; fry for a while, then add ½ cup water and cook until the water evaporates and the cauliflower is half cooked. (Do not overcook it). Add coriander and lemon juice, mix well, cool the mixture.

Roll out the dough and cut rounds; on one round put some cauliflower mixture and cover with another round, sealing the sides well, make all the purees in this way and fry in hot oil, drain on paper and serve hot with the chilli sauce.

Will serve twelve people.

Chilli Sauce:

2 tbsp oil	½ tsp mustard seeds
½ tsp methi seeds	½ cup jaggery
1 cup thick tamarind pulp	12 green chillies, more if liked
1 tsp salt	

Mix jaggery with the tamarind pulp and strain.

Heat oil, add mustard and methi seeds, then chopped green chillies. Fry a little, then add salt and tamarind mixture, give one boil and cool.

CAPSICUM IN CURDS

12 capsicums	½ kilo curds
2 tbsp cummin	1 dsp salt
1 large bunch coriander	oil

Grind cummin, coriander and salt with a little lemon juice.

Wash capsicums and slit on one side, and remove the seeds, then apply the ground masala inside each capsicum.

Heat ½ cup oil and fry the capsicums on all sides in it.

Just before serving, drain all the water from the curds and add to the fried capsicums. Stir over low heat. Do not boil. Serve immediately.

Will serve six to eight people.

CAPSICUM IN MASALA

½ kilo capsicum	1 tbsp sesame seeds
3 red chillies	1 tbsp jaggery
1 tsp cummin	½ cup oil
1 tbsp tamarind	1 tsp salt
½ grated coconut	

Wash capsicum and cut into four, remove the cluster of seeds then fry in oil, remove from the oil, and to the oil add ground masala (coconut, chillies, sesame and cummin seeds).

Mix jaggery and tamarind to 1 cup water, when the jaggery is melted, strain the liquid, and add to the masala, add salt, cook on slow fire until oil floats on top, then add fried capsicums, mix and serve sprinkled with some chopped roasted peanuts.

Will serve four to six people.

VEGETABLE SALNOO

3 potatoes	1 brinjal
2 sweet potatoes	3 carrots
1 cup greenpeas, boiled	1 small cauliflower
1 cup chopped french beans	4 onions
12 green chillies, chopped	1 piece ginger, chopped
12 slices garlic, chopped	1 tsp cummin
1 tsp turmeric	1 dsp chilli powder
½ tsp mustard seeds	1 tbsp dhanajeera
1 large bunch coriander	½ cup grated coconut
juice of 3 lemons	1 dsp salt

Cut all the vegetables in cubes and fry in oil, remove and in ½ cup of the same oil fry chopped onions to golden brown, then add ginger, garlic, chillies and all the dry spices; fry for a while, then add all the fried vegetables and mix well, add lemon juice; chopped coriander and ½ cup water. Cook on slow fire until all the water is absorbed by the vegetables and the oil floats on top.

Will serve six to eight people.

RED PUMPKIN STEW

1 kilo red pumpkin, peeled and cut into small cubes	1 tbs jaggery
	6 slices garlic
	8 red chillies
4 chopped onions	1 dsp tamarind
1 piece ginger	½ cup oil
½ coconut	1 dsp salt

Soak tamarind in ½ cup hot water, then squeeze and strain the juice.

Grind chillies, garlic, ginger and coconut to a fine paste.

Fry onions in oil until golden brown, add ground masala and salt, fry well, mix well and add cubed pumpkins, and ½ cup water, cook on slow fire until the pumpkin is cooked, then add jaggery and the tamarind juice and cook until the oil floats on top. Serve sprinkled with chopped coriander.

Will serve six to eight people.

MASALA OKHRA

½ kilo okhra (bhendi)
1 bunch coriander
2 tbsp besan
6 green chillies

1 dsp dhanajeera
½ dsp salt
juice of 2 lemons

Wash the okhras and keep them whole, just slit them on one side.

Melt 2 tbsp oil, add chopped chillies and besan and fry for a while, then add dhanajeera, salt and chopped coriander and mix all. Fill the okhras with this mixture.

Heat 4 tbsp of oil and place all the okhras in it, keep it on slow fire, some water may be kept on the lid, but must not be added to the okhras. When they are cooked, sprinkle with lemon juice and serve.

Will serve four to six people.

BRINJAL SALNOO

1 kilo brinjals
12 slices garlic
1 dsp cummin
4 green chillies
1 tbsp coriander seeds
1 cup oil

8 red chillies
1 small piece ginger
12 curry leaves
1 cup vinegar
2 tbsp jaggery
1 dsp salt

Wash brinjals, dry and cut into cubes and fry them in hot oil.

Grind to a fine paste in vinegar, chillies, garlic, cummin, and coriander. After frying all the brinjals, in the same oil (add a little more if needed), fry the chopped green chillies and curry leaves, then add the ground masala and fry until the oil separates, then add jaggery, when it melts add the fried brinjals and any of the remaining vinegar. Keep on slow fire until the oil floats on top. Sprinkle with chopped coriander.

Will serve eight to ten people.

DAL CUTLETS

*1 cup red lentils
  (masoor dal)*
6 green chillies
½ tsp pepper
½ tsp chilli powder
3 onions
breadcrumbs

oil
3 potatoes
1 bunch coriander
1 dsp salt
1 tbsp W. sauce
2 eggs

Soak lentils for an hour, then boil in just enough water to cover; when the lentils are cooked and the water is completely dried, mash it well. Boil potatoes and mash.

Chop onions and fry in oil until brown, chop chillies and coriander. Mix dal, potatoes, chillies, coriander, salt, pepper, chilli powder, W. sauce and fried onions; mix all well and form into cutlets, dip them in eggs and in breadcrumbs and fry in oil.

For vegetarians, who do not eat eggs, dip the cutlets in a batter made from besan and water, and then roll in breadcrumbs.

Will serve six to eight people.

CAULIFLOWER FRITTERS

1 large cauliflower
1 cup flour
1 tbsp salad oil
3 eggs

1 cup milk
½ cup grated cheese
oil for frying
½ tsp baking powder

Parboil cauliflower in salt water, then separate the buds.

Separate yolks from whites and then beat the yolks with 1 tsp salt, pepper, chilli powder; gradually add sifted flour (sifted with ½ tsp baking powder) and milk and make a smooth batter; add cheese and salad oil; leave the mixture for half an hour, then dip the cauliflower buds in the batter and fry in hot oil until golden. Serve hot.

Will serve six to eight people.

CHEESE AND CHUTNEY TOASTS

Chutney:

½ coconut
1 bunch coriander
1 tsp sugar
½ tsp salt

4 green chillies
1 tsp cummin
juice of 1 lemon

Grind all the above ingredients to a fine paste.

Cheese Sauce:

1 cup grated cheese
2 tbsp butter
½ tsp salt

2 cups milk
4 tbsp flour
½ tsp pepper

Make thick cheese sauce from the above ingredients.
Fry 8 slices of bread.
Spread chutney on fried bread slices, put in a flat dish
and cover with cheese sauce, put under a griller to brown
the top. Serve hot immediately.
If preferred, a slice of bacon can be put over the
cheese sauce before grilling.
Will serve eight people.

CARROT RINGS WITH CREAMED PEAS

2 cups grated carrots
1 cup milk
2 tbsp salad oil
½ cup breadcrumbs

2 eggs
1 tsp salt
½ tsp pepper

Mix carrots with breadcrumbs; add salt and pepper.
Beat lightly eggs with milk and salad oil, add the carrot mixture to it. Grease a ring mould and fill it with
the carrot mixture. Put the mould in hot water and bake
in a slow oven until firm. Unmould on a plate and fill
with peas sauce.

Peas Sauce:

1 cup milk	1 tbsp butter
1 tbsp flour	½ kilo green peas
½ tsp salt	½ tsp pepper
½ tsp chilli powder	2 dsp W. sauce

Melt butter, add flour, fry a little then add 1 cup hot milk, stir until it boils, season it and add boiled peas, and pour hot into the carrot mould. A little grated cheese may be added, if liked, to the sauce.

Any other filling, with eggs, fish or chicken can be used.

Will serve eight to ten people.

CARROT SOUFFLE

2 cups boiled and mash- ed carrots	Few drops tobasco or chilli sauce
2 tbsp flour	1 cup milk
3 eggs	4 tbsp butter
1 tsp salt	1 dsp sugar
½ tsp pepper	1 tbsp W. sauce

Melt butter add flour and hot milk and make a white sauce; to this add carrot pulp and seasonings, bring to boil, stirring constantly. Cool the mixture, then beat in egg yolks, then fold in stiffly beaten egg whites. Mix well and pour into a greased souffle dish and bake in a hot oven until well risen and firm. Serve immediately.

Will serve eight to ten people.

GLAZED CARROTS WITH ONIONS

½ kilo baby carrots	¾ cup brown sugar
4 tbs butter	2 tbsp lemon juice
1 tsp nutmeg	1 tsp salt
1 tbsp chopped parsley	½ tsp pepper
½ kilo small onions	

Parboil carrots and onions, then drain them and add the other ingredients, toss them over slow fire, until sugar melts. Serve, sprinkled with parsley.
Will serve four to six people.

GREENPEAS IN ORANGE JUICE

1 kilo greenpeas	1 tbsp grated orange rind
¾ cup orange juice	2 tbsp butter
2 tbsp chopped fresh	1 tsp salt
mint	½ tsp pepper

Boil peas and drain. Melt butter and add chopped mint and orange rind, saute for 2 minutes, then add sugar, seasonings and orange juice; stir all, then add greenpeas and bring to boil. Serve hot.
Will serve six to eight people.

BAKED CHEESE FONDUE

4 slices bread cut into	1 tsp salt, ½ tsp pepper
cubes	2 cups milk
1 cup any cheese cut	2 tbsp butter
into cubes	½ tsp mustard
3 eggs	¼ tsp chilli powder

Soak bread cubes in milk for 10 minutes, add cheese cubes. Beat egg yolks with seasonings and add to the bread mixture, mix well. Beat egg whites stiffly and fold into the bread mixture. Pour into a well greased dish and bake in a hot oven, until set and golden on top. Serve immediately.
This dish can be prepared and kept, but the egg whites must be folded just before baking.
Will serve six to eight people.

CORN RAREBIT

2 cups frozen corn	2 tbsp butter
2 onions finely chopped	1 cup grated cheese
6 large slices bread	1 tsp salt, ½ tsp pepper
¼ tsp chilli powder	1 tbsp W. sauce

Put corn in hot water and boil, then drain.

Melt butter and fry the onions until golden, then add flour, milk and corn and bring all to a boil, stir until smooth, add cheese and seasonings.

Fry lightly bread slices in butter, then pour corn mixture over each toast, put some slices of hardboiled eggs or slices of capsicum over it and serve hot.

Pieces of ham or chicken can be added to the corn mixture, if desired.

Will serve four to six people.

HARRICOT LOAF

2 cups harricot beans	½ cup chopped onions
3 green chillies	2 tbsp coriander
½ tsp chilli powder	1 dsp salt, ½ tsp pepper
1 cup breadcrumbs	2 eggs
½ cup milk	½ cup tomato ketchup
1 tbsp W. sauce	

Soak beans overnight in water, next morning wash them and boil them until tender, drain the water and run through a mincer.

Fry onions in 2 tbsp of butter and mix this with all the other ingredients to the harricot beans paste. Mix well and put it in a well greased loaf pan. Put the pan in water and bake in a moderate oven until done. Unmould and garnish with any vegetable. Serve with tomato ketchup.

Will serve six to eight people.

VEGETABLE PUFFS

2 cups flour	2 tbsp coriander chopped
2 tsp baking powder	2 cups mixed boiled
6 green chillies chopped	vegetables like peas,
¼ tsp chilli powder	carrots, frenchbeans,
1 cup milk	potatoes and cauli-
1 dsp salt, ½ tsp pepper	flower

Sift flour and baking powder together. Beat eggs slightly and add to the milk; add this gradually to the flour and make a batter, then add all the other ingredients and mix well. Heat oil and drop the vegetable mixture by spoonfulls and fry a nice brown. Serve hot with tomato ketchup or green chutney.
Will serve eight to ten people.

POTATO SALNOO

1 kilo potatoes	*12 green chillies*
1 tbsp sambhar	*1 tbsp chilli powder*
1 tsp turmeric	*15 curry leaves*
1 cup sweet oil	*juice of two lemons*
1 dsp salt	

Peel and cut potatoes into small cubes. Chop chillies. Heat oil and add chillies, take it off the fire and add sambhar chilli powder, turmeric, curry leaves and salt; mix all, add potatoes, mix well with the masala, then put the pan in a moderate oven and mix once or twice; when cooked, add lemon juice and serve, sprinkled with chopped coriander. Serve with chapatties or purees.
Few roasted cashewnuts can be added to the above salnoo.
Will serve six to eight people.

POTATOES AND DRY FRUIT STEW

4 large potatoes	*½ cup raisins*
½ cup sliced almonds	*¼ cup pistachio*
¼ cup charoli	*1 cup dry apricots*
4 large onions	*6 green chillies*
1 large bunch coriander	*½ coconut*
1 tsp chilli powder	*1 tsp turmeric*
1 tsp pepper	*1 dsp sugar*
juice of 2 lemons	*1 dsp salt, oil*

Peel potatoes and grate them as for straw potatoes. Fry them in hot oil, remove and keep aside.
Slice onions finely, grate coconut, chop chillies and coriander.

Wash raisins and apricots, chop almonds and pistachio.

Heat $\frac{1}{2}$ cup oil and fry the onions until golden brown; then to it add chillies, coriander, coconut, chilli powder, turmeric, salt and pepper and fry all for a while; then add all dried fruits and nuts and mix well, add $\frac{1}{2}$ cup water and let it cook on slow fire until the water dries up, then add fried straw potatoes, add sugar and lemon juice, mix well and keep on slow fire for a while until oil separates.

Will serve eight to ten people.

SAMBHAR POTATOES

1 kilo small potatoes	12 curry leaves
1 tsp turmeric	1 dsp - sambhar
1 tsp chilli powder	6 green chillies
oil	

Boil potatoes, peel and fry them in oil until golden.

Heat 2 tbsp oil, add chopped chillies and curry leaves, fry for 2 minutes, take it off the fire, add other spices, and salt (if the sambhar is not salty), add potatoes; keep on slow fire for 10 minutes. Serve, sprinkled with chopped coriander.

Will serve six to eight people.

POTATO TART

1 kilo potatoes	4 tbs butter
$\frac{1}{4}$ cup sliced onions	$\frac{1}{4}$ cup sliced capsicums
$\frac{1}{4}$ cup sliced celery	$\frac{1}{4}$ cup chopped gherkins
1 cup cream	$\frac{1}{2}$ cup milk
2 eggs, 2 egg yolks	1 cup grated cheese
1 tsp grated nutmeg	1 dsp salt, $\frac{1}{2}$ tsp pepper

Boil potatoes and mash them with 2 tbs flour, 2 tbs butter, salt, pepper and nutmeg. Make into a dough and line a greased 9″ pie dish.

Melt 2 tbs butter on a pan, add onions, capsicum and celery saute until soft, not brown. Remove from fire add gherkin and pour it all in the potato-lined dish.

Beat eggs and egg yolks lightly and season with salt
and pepper, add milk and cream; pour this over the
vegetable mixture, sprinkle cheese and nutmeg over it.
Bake in a moderate oven for about 40 min. or until set.
Serve hot.
Will serve six to eight people.

GLAZED SWEET POTATOES

1 kilo sweet potatoes	*1 cup brown sugar*
½ cup water	*¼ tsp salt*
4 tbsp butter	*1 tsp ground cinnamon*
¼ cup chopped walnuts	

Parboil potatoes, peel and cut them into pieces.
Mix sugar, water, salt, and butter in a large fry pan,
bring to boil stir until sugar melts, then lay the sweet
potato pieces in the syrup, and let it cook on slow fire,
turning the potatoes to glaze all over and until cooked.
Before serving, sprinkle them with walnuts and cinnamon.
Will serve six to eight people.

SWEET POTATO AND DATE BAKE

1 kilo sweet potato	*1 cup chopped dates*
1 cup light cream	*4 tbsp butter*
2 tsp cinnamon	*½ tsp salt*
2 tbsp chopped walnuts	

Boil potatoes, peel and mash. To this add all the
other ingredients except walnuts. Mix all well, turn into
a greased baking dish and bake in a moderate oven for
about 20 min.; then sprinkle with walnuts and bake until
brown on top.
Will serve ten to twelve people.

SWEET POTATO AND ORANGE BAKE

½ kilo sweet potato	*2 tbsp butter*
½ cup orange juice	*1 tbsp chopped orange*
½ tsp salt	*rind*
1 tbsp rum	*1 tsp grated nutmeg*

Boil potatoes, peel and mash. Add all the other ingredients and bake in a moderate oven until brown on top. *Will serve six to eight people.*

POTATO CHEESE RISSOLES

6 *large potatoes*	1 *cup cheese*
1 *tsp salt*, ½ *tsp pepper*	½ *tsp chilli powder*
3 *eggs*	¼ *cup milk*
breadcrumbs, oil	

Boil potatoes and mash them, add cheese, seasonings and hot milk, make into a pliable paste. Shape into rissoles, dip them in beaten eggs and roll them in fine breadcrumbs. Fry them in deep oil until golden brown. Serve hot sprinkled with some cheese and chopped coriander.
Will serve eight to ten people.

POTATO OMELETTE

2 *potatoes*	½ *tsp nutmeg*
2 *tbsp butter*	3 *eggs*
½ *tsp salt*, ¼ *tsp pepper*	1 *tbs lemon juice*

Boil potatoes and mash, add butter, egg yolks, salt, pepper and nutmeg. Beat egg whites stiff and fold in the potato mixture.

Heat 2 to 3 tbs of oil in a large fry pan and pour the potato mixture in it, close the lid and let it cook on slow fire; when brown and set, turn and let the other side brown, or put it under a griller to brown the top. Serve immediately.

If liked, 2 tbsp cheese or a few chopped chillies may be added.
Will serve four to six people.

SOUFFLE POTATOES

4 *large potatoes*   *oil for frying*
salt

Peel the potatoes, wash and dry with a cloth, then slice them into $\frac{1}{4}''$ thick slices.

Heat the oil and fry a few slices at a time for a few minutes, then drain them on paper, when all the potatoes are fried, let them get cold.

Before serving heat the oil until it smokes then add a few potatoes at a time and fry until they puff. Drain and sprinkle with fine salt.

Will serve four to six people.

POTATO PANCAKES

4 *large potatoes*   2 *green chillies*
2 *large finely sliced*   2 *tbsp flour*
  onions   1 *tsp nutmeg grated*
3 *eggs*   *oil for frying*
1 *dsp salt*, $\frac{1}{2}$ *tsp pepper*

Peel the potatoes and grate them fine, add to it sliced onions, chopped green chillies, flour, seasonings and lightly beaten eggs, mix all this well.

Heat oil in a fry pan, take one tsp of the potato mixture and put in oil, flattening it to a round. Fry until golden brown on both sides. Serve hot.

These pancakes can be served with apple sauce. Chillies can be omitted.

For vegetarians, omit eggs and add 3 tbsp besan flour instead of plain flour.

Will serve six to eight people.

BAKED POTATOES WITH STUFFING

6 *large baked potatoes* $\frac{1}{2}$ *cup milk*
4 *tbsp butter*   1 *egg well beaten*
1 *dsp salt* $\frac{1}{2}$ *tsp pepper*

Cut the baked potatoes into halves, scoop out the pulp, leaving a $\frac{1}{4}''$ shell. Mash the pulp adding milk, butter, salt and pepper; fold in the beaten egg. Refill the mixture into the shells, pile high and scour with a fork, bake in a hot oven until the top is brown. Serve hot.

If liked, sprinkle some cheese over it whilst baking. For more cheesy potatoes, add 1 cup cheese to the potatoes before filling the shells.

Will serve six people.

DIFFERENT STUFFING FOR BAKED POTATOES

crisply fried bacon
chopped ham or tongue
prawns or crab meat
hardboiled eggs, olives,

sardines, pimento
grated nutmeg or cinnamon

RICE AND CURRY

Rice is the staple diet of our people, more so in the South where almost everything is made from rice.

Every family has rice on its menu every day.

Unmilled rice is very good nutritionally, but we prefer white rice as it looks more appetising. There are so many varieties of rice but in most of the good rice dishes such as Biryani and Pulao, we always use long-grained Delhi or Basmati rice.

Basmati rice, if soaked for an hour before cooking, becomes longer and fluffier.

Rice should be added when the water has come to a boil, and not from the beginning in cold water.

1 tsp of lemon juice to boiling rice keeps the rice white.

1 cupful of raw rice approximately equals 3 to 3½ cups when cooked.

If the rice is new, then one has to be careful, as a little overcooking makes it lumpy.

Old rice, which has been stored for some time, is the best, as the grains keep separate, and it absorbs more water.

As soon as the rice is cooked, it should be poured into a collander, all the water drained, and a little cold water run over it, so that it will not become soft.

When reheating rice, a little water should be sprinkled over it and kept on a very slow fire. A heat deflector may be used, as the heat will spread evenly on the bottom of the pan.

Curries are the speciality of our country.

Curries can be hot as well as mild, chillies must be adjusted to taste, any fish, meat, eggs or vegetables can be added to the curry.

The curry masala must be ground very fine, to make a good curry.

If the curry masala is made in a blender, which many housewives do these days, it is better that it is strained before making the curry.

Curry masala must be fried well in oil, then coconut milk or water must be added.

A curry must be simmered on very low heat, until the oil floats on top.

ARABIAN PULAO

1 kilo mutton
1 kilo ghee
1 piece ginger
1 dsp garam masala
1 tbsp almonds or
  cashew
2 tbsp raisins
½ tsp saffron
juice of 1 lemon

1 kilo Delhi rice
4 onions
12 slices garlic
1 tbs shahjeera (black
  cummin)
1 tbsp pistachio
3 hardboiled eggs
1 dsp salt
½ kilo curds

Roast saffron lightly and soak it in lemon juice.

Cut meat into pieces, apply ground ginger and garlic, add curds to it, mix well and keep the mutton in the marinade for at least two hours or if possible overnight. Then melt 3 tbsp ghee, remove the mutton from the marinade and fry in ghee; when fried brown, add all the marinade and let the mutton cook until tender.

Parboil rice with 1 dsp salt, drain. Mix a quarter of rice with the saffron soaked in lemon juice.

Chop onions and fry to a golden, drain and keep aside.

Pour ¼ cup of oil in which the onions were fried in a large pan, put in half of the white rice, over it put half of the saffron rice, then sprinkle with half of the garam masala and half fried onions, then put all the mutton over it, sprinkle a little of the garam masala, layer again with saffron rice, white rice, fried onions and garam masala. Pour the remaining melted ghee over it all. Make a paste with some flour and water and seal the lid with it. Put in a slow oven for about an hour, or until the rice is cooked.

Serve garnished with hardboiled eggs, fried nuts and raisins and some fried onions.

Will serve ten to twelve people.

MUTTON PULAO

1 kilo mutton
½ kilo curds
4 potatoes
8 green chillies
1 piece ginger
12 mint leaves
2 pieces cinnamon
12 cardamom
1 cup ghee
1 dsp salt

1 kilo Delhi rice
6 onions
1 bunch coriander
12 slices garlic
1 tsp shahjeera
½ tsp saffron
½ nutmeg
6 peppercorns
1 tbsp sweet oil

Cut mutton into pieces. Grind coriander, chillies, garlic, ginger, mint and cummins to a paste and apply to the mutton and keep for two hours.

Parboil rice with salt and sweet oil. Drain and keep aside.

Chop onions finely, and fry in oil and keep aside.

Pound to powder shahjeera, nutmeg, cardamom, cinnamon and peppercorn.

Drain the curds and remove the water; to this add half of the pounded masala.

Soak saffron in the juice of one lemon.

Add 3 cups water to the mutton and cook until tender and one cup gravy remains; add pieces of potatoes and cook until potatoes are half cooked, add saffron to the curds, mix well, add two cups of parboiled rice to it.

Put half cup oil in a large pan, put in it half of the white rice, and half of the saffron rice, sprinkle half of the garam masala, half of the fried onions, then all the mutton mixture, cover with remaining saffron rice and then the remaining white rice, sprinkle with remaining garam masala and fried onions. Pour over it any remaining fried oil. Seal the pan and keep in a slow oven for an hour or until the rice is cooked. Sprinkle with fried onions and serve.

Will serve ten to twelve people.

MINCED MEAT PULAO

2 cups rice	1 cup tur dal
¼ kilo ghee	6 onions
12 slices garlic	1 piece ginger
12 green chillies	1 large bunch coriander
1 tsp cummin	1 tsp shahjeera
1 dsp garam masala	1 kilo mutton (minced)
1 dsp salt	2 onions

Grind garlic, ginger, chillies, coriander and apply to the mutton mince, leave for about two hours.

Parboil rice with 1 dsp salt, and drain.

Wash dal and soak in 2 cups water for an hour, then add 1 tsp salt and boil until cooked and all the water is absorbed, leave the dal whole, do not mush it up.

Melt 4 tbsp of ghee and fry the sliced onions crisp in it, remove and keep aside, in the same ghee add a little more ghee and fry the marinated mince, when fried brown, add ½ cup water and let it cook over slow fire, until dry and all the water is absorbed, then mix the mince with the cooked dal.

Pound cummin, shahjeera and mix with the other garam masala.

Put some melted ghee in a large pan and put 1|3 of parboiled rice in it, over it put half the mince and dal mixture, sprinkle with 1|3 of the fried onions and 1|3 of the pounded spices; repeat the layers, ending with rice; sprinkle some fried onions and spices on top, pour over it the remaining melted ghee and put the pan in a slow oven, until the rice is cooked. Serve hot in layers, do not mix at all up.

Serve curd chutney with it.

Will serve ten to twelve people.

TOMATO RICE

2 cups Delhi rice	1 kilo red ripe tomatoes
6 onions	2 dsp sugar
1 dsp garam masala	1 dsp salt
1 tsp chilli powder	1 tsp cummin
½ cup tomato ketchup	4 tbsp ghee
4 green chillies	1 bunch coriander

Wash rice and soak for an hour.

Blanch tomatoes in hot water, peel and chop. Chop chillies and coriander. Slice onions finely and fry in ghee until golden, remove half of it from the ghee; to the rest add chillies, coriander, cummin, salt, mixed spices, sugar and tomatoes; mix all well, then add rice and fry for a while, until the tomato water dries up. Then add tomato ketchup and 2 cups water. Let the rice cook on slow fire until the rice is cooked, add more hot water if needed. Do not add too much water at a time.

Serve sprinkled with fried onions.

The rice is served with plain masala dal and small mutton kababs.

Will serve six to eight people.

VEGETABLE RICE

4 cups Delhi rice	½ cup masoor dal
1 coconut	2 potatoes
1 sweet potato	2 carrots
4 tomatoes	¼ kilo bhendi
¼ kilo green peas	6 onions
2 cooking bananas	1 dsp dhanajeera
1 tsp turmeric	1 tsp cummin
12 peppercorns	1 piece cinnamon
4 cloves	10 green chillies
1 big bunch coriander	12 slices garlic
1 piece ginger	1 dsp salt

Wash rice and soak for an hour.

Grate the coconut, leave half and extract two cups milk from the other half. Chop tomatoes.

Cut into cubes potatoes, sweet potatoes, and carrots, slice bhendis, fry each separately in oil, sprinkle with a little salt water, fry crisp. Boil green peas, slice bananas and fry.

Chop 3 onions finely and fry in oil until golden, then add to it chopped chillies, ginger, garlic, coriander, cummin, grated coconut, cloves, peppercorns, cinnamon, salt and chopped tomatoes, and fry for a while; then add dal, mix all well, add coconut milk and let it cook until the rice is cooked, add a little water if needed. Then add all the fried vegetables except bananas.

Fry the 3 remaining sliced onions in oil until crisp and golden, sprinkle over rice before serving and also lay the fried bananas over it.

Will serve about fifteen to twenty people.

RICE MATADOR

4 cups rice	1 kilo tomatoes
12 slices garlic	1 cup sliced mushrooms
1 cup cucumbers	½ cup chopped capsicum
1 cup olive oil	2 cups grated cheese
1 cup chopped celery	1 tsp pepper
1 dsp salt	basil or marjoram if
1 tsp roasted cummin	available
4 onions	

Boil rice with 1 dsp salt and drain, do not overcook it, it should be a little undercooked.

Heat oil and fry mushrooms, then remove and fry chopped onions until golden brown, add chopped garlic and cucumber and fry for 5 min. then add capsicum, tomatoes cut into fours and seasonings, then add rice and mix well.

Grease a casserol and make layers of rice with mushrooms and cheese in between the rice. Sprinkle the top finally with some cheese. Bake in a hot oven for 30 min. just before serving.

Serve with hot tomato gravy.

Basil or marjoram may be omitted.

Will serve twelve to fifteen people.

RICE JAMBALAYA

2 cups Delhi rice	6 slices garlic
4 tomatoes	4 green chillies
1 piece ginger	½ cup sliced mushrooms
1 cup boiled green peas	1 cup shelled boiled
¼ kilo cocktail sausages	prawns
½ tsp chilli powder	1 dsp salt
½ tsp pepper	1 cup butter or oil
3 onions	

Boil rice in salted water, drain and run cold water over it so that it will not soften more.

Chop onions and garlic and fry in 2 tbsp butter until golden.

Slice mushrooms and fry in 1 tbsp butter.

Fry prawns in one tbsp butter until pink.

Boil sausages in water and drain.

Wash tomatoes, remove the top and cut each into eight wedges.

To the fried onions and garlic, add tomatoes and fry for a while, then add chopped chillies; add all this to the boiled rice along with peas, prawns, mushrooms, sausages and season well. Mix everything together and put the pan on a very slow fire for about ½ hour before serving, to absorb flavours. Serve hot.

Will serve eight to ten people.

RICE AND CHILLI BAKE

2 cups rice	½ kilo mutton mince
8 green chillies	½ kilo tomatoes
4 onions	¼ cup oil or butter
1 dsp salt	1 tsp chilli powder
1 dsp sugar	

Parboil rice with salt, drain and run cold water over it keep it aside.

Chop onions, chillies and tomatoes.

Heat oil and fry onions until brown, add chillies and the mutton mince, keep frying until the mince is dry, then add tomatoes, sugar and salt, stir well, then add rice and mix well.

Grease a baking dish and pour the rice mixture in it. Bake in a moderate oven for about 30 min. Serve hot.

Capsicums can be used instead of chillies.

Will serve eight to ten people.

SUPER KHICHDI

2 cups Delhi rice	½ cup masoor dal
1 coconut	6 green chillies
1 large bunch coriander	12 slices garlic
1 piece ginger	1 tsp turmeric
2 tsp dhanajeera	1 tsp cummin
1 piece cinnamon	6 cloves
6 cardamoms	4 large onions
2 potatoes	2 tbsp raisins
2 tbsp cashew nuts	½ cup ghee or oil
1 dsp salt	2 dsp sugar

Soak rice for an hour, then wash it along with the dal.
Slice onions finely, chop chillies, coriander, ginger and
garlic. Pound cummin, cinnamon, cloves and cardamoms.

Grate coconut, leave a quarter aside and extract 3 cups
milk from the rest.

Fry onions in oil until golden, remove half of the fried
onions and keep it aside. To the onions add ginger, garlic, chillies, coriander, coconut and pounded spices, fry
all this for a while, until it all browns. Then add turmeric, dhanajeera, salt and rice and dal, mix all well then
add coconut milk and 1 cup water, cook on slow fire,
when the rice is half cooked, add pieces of potatoes, let
it cook until the rice is tender; a little more hot water
may be added gradually, if needed, do not make the rice
too soft.

Serve sprinkled with fried onions, raisins and cashewnuts.

Will serve ten to twelve people.

SHEEKH CURRY

1 kilo mutton, or beef cut into cubes	4 tbsp oil
	2 potatoes
3 large onions	1 piece ginger
12 slices garlic	1 dsp cummin
1 coconut	2 dsp coriander seeds
1 tsp turmeric	12 curry leaves
12 red chillies	juice of 3 lemons
1 dsp salt	a few slit green chillies

Grind ginger and garlic, apply to the meat cubes and leave for an hour. If possible, leave it overnight in the refrigerator.

Cut potatoes and onions in cubes.

Skewer the meat on the skewers alternately with potatoes and onions.

Grind half the coconut with chillies, cummin, turmeric and coriander to a very fine paste. Extract 2 cups of milk from the other half coconut.

Chop one onion finely and fry golden in oil, then add curry leaves and fry them; add the ground masala and fry well until the oil separates; then add the skewered meat and fry for a while; add salt and coconut milk, and 2 cups water; let the curry simmer over low heat until the meat is done, add a little hot water if necessary; lastly, add lemon juice and slit chillies, let it simmer for a while and serve.

Will serve eight to ten people.

DRY MUTTON CURRY

1 kilo mutton	2 coconuts
25 red goa chillies	12 green chillies
2 tbsp coriander seeds	2 tbsp poppy seeds
1 tbsp cummin	12 slices garlic
6 cloves	1 piece cinnamon
1 tsp turmeric	4 onions
15 curry leaves	juice of 3 lemons
2 tbsp cashewnuts	2 tbsp raisins or currants

Wash mutton and cut into small pieces, make two cups stock from the bones.

Roast chillies, coriander seeds, poppyseeds and cummin, then grind to a paste with grated coconuts, garlic, cinnamon and cloves and turmeric.

Melt 6 tbsp of oil and fry cashew and raisins, remove, and in the same oil fry finely chopped onions to golden brown, then add curry leaves, whole green chillies and the ground masala; then fry until the masala is brown, then add small pieces of mutton and keep frying; then add a little stock at a time and let the mutton cook on a slow fire; do not add too much stock at a time. If needed, a little hot water may be added until the mutton is tender, then add lemon juice. Just before serving, add fried nuts and raisins.

This curry is hot and spicy. Serve it with plain white rice and plain dal.

Chillies may be adjusted to taste.

Will serve eight to ten people.

KHURMA CURRY

1 kilo mutton	1 coconut
12 red chillies	2 tbsp roasted peanuts
4 onions	2 tbsp channa
2 dsp coriander seeds	2 tbsp poppyseeds
15 slices garlic	1 dsp chopped ginger
4 cloves	1 piece cinnamon
1 bunch coriander leaves	1 dsp salt
1 tbsp sugar	½ kilo curds
4 tbsp oil	

Cut mutton into pieces and boil until half cooked, and 1 cup stock remains. Grind ½ coconut with all the above ingredients except sugar and curds. Extract one cup milk from the other half coconut.

Will serve eight to ten people.

VINDALOO CURRY

1 kilo pork	12 red chillies
12 slices garlic	1 tbsp minced ginger
1 dsp cummin	1 dsp mustard seeds
1 tsp turmeric	4 cloves
1 piece cinnamon	4 cardamoms
3 onions	1 tbsp tamarind
½ cup vinegar	1 coconut
1 dsp salt	2 tbsp oil
a few green chillies	

Grate the coconut, add 4 cups hot water and extract milk.

Chop ginger and garlic.

Grind chillies, cummin, mustard, turmeric, cloves, cinnamon and cardamom in vinegar.

Mix the ground masala, ginger and garlic with the pork cubes and leave in the refrigerator overnight (if possible) or for about 2 hours.

Soak tamarind in half cup vinegar, and strain the pulp.

Next day, slice onions and fry in oil until brown, then add the marinated pork, coconut milk and salt, simmer until pork is well cooked. Add tamarind pulp, and simmer for another 10 minutes.

A few green chillies may be added, if desired.

Will serve eight to ten people.

VEGETABLE CURRY

1 coconut	12 red chillies
1 dsp coriander seeds	1 tsp turmeric
1 dsp cummin	12 slices garlic
1 piece ginger	12 curry leaves
1 tbsp tamarind	1 dsp salt
4 large onions	100 gm french beans
100 gm green peas	100 gm carrots
100 gm okhra (bhendi)	2 potatoes
4 tbsp oil	

Grate coconut and grind the quarter of the coconut with chillies, coriander, cummin, garlic, ginger and turmeric. To the rest of the coconut, add 2 cups hot water and extract milk, add tamarind to the milk and leave aside for some time, then strain the milk.

Cut all the vegetables into small pieces. Heat 1 cup oil and fry all the vegetables, each one separately; keep aside. In the same oil fry chopped onions until brown, then add ground masala, salt and curry leaves, fry well until oil separates, add two cups water and the green peas, let it simmer until the peas are tender, add coconut and tamarind mixture and all the fried vegetables, simmer on slow fire until oil floats on top.

Heat oil and fry the ground masala until brown and the oil separates, then add mutton with one cup stock and the coconut milk; simmer over low heat until thick and oil floats on top, and the mutton is well cooked. Just before serving, drain water from curds and beat it

well, add to the hot curry with sugar. Stir and serve
immediately. Do not boil again.

This curry can also be made with chicken.

Will serve eight to ten people.

CHICKEN CURRY

1 chicken	1½ coconuts
2 onions	8 red chillies
½ pod garlic	1 piece ginger
1 dsp cummin	1 dsp coriander seeds
1 tsp turmeric	6 green chillies
12 curry leaves	½ cup oil
1 dsp salt	juice of 2 lemons

Parboil the chicken with salt and a piece of ginger,
and leave one cup stock.

Grate one coconut, add 3 cups of hot water and extract
milk.

Grate ½ coconut and grind with chillies, garlic, cummin,
coriander and turmeric to a paste.

Chop onions finely and fry in oil until brown; then add
the ground masala; curry leaves and slit green chillies;
fry until the oil separates and the masala is well browned,
then add the coconut milk and the chicken stock, and
salt; boil for 10 minutes, then add chicken pieces and
let the curry simmer until the chicken is cooked and oil
floats on top, then add lemon juice.

Will serve six to eight people.

VINEGARY CHICKEN CURRY

1 chicken	1½ coconuts
15 red chillies	2 tbs coriander
1 dsp cummin	12 slices garlic
1 piece ginger	1 tsp turmeric
2 onions	6 curry leaves
1 dsp salt	vinegar

Parboil chicken with salt, a piece of ginger and leave 2 cups stock.

Grate ½ coconut and grind to a very fine paste in vinegar with chillies, coriander, cummin, garlic and turmeric.

Chop onion finely and fry in 3 tbs oil to a golden brown; add curry leaves, then the ground paste and fry until brown, and oil separates, add the coconut milk, stock and chicken pieces. Simmer until the chicken is cooked and the curry is thick, add ½ cup vinegar and 1 dsp sugar before serving.

Will serve six to eight people.

TOMATO CHICKEN CURRY

1 chicken	1 kilo red ripe tomatoes
1 large coconut	4 onions
1 tsp cummin	12 red chillies
12 slices garlic	1 tbs coriander
12 peppercorns	1 dsp salt
2 dsp sugar	1 piece ginger
juice of 2 lemons	½ cup oil
½ tsp saffron	

Grate coconut and grind half of it with chillies, coriander, cummin, garlic, peppercorns and ginger.

Add 2 cups hot water to the remaining half of the grated coconut and extract milk.

Parboil chicken and leave 2 cups stock.

Blanch the tomatoes, skin them and chop finely, then add this to the coconut milk, leave for an hour and strain it through a sieve, to this add saffron and keep aside.

Chop onions finely and fry golden in oil, to this add the ground masala and fry well, then add sugar and salt; then add tomato coconut mixture, let it simmer on slow fire until thick, then add chicken and stock and simmer until the required thickness, and until the oil floats on top. Add lemon juice and serve.

Will serve six to eight people.

FISH CURRY

2 pomfrets or any other
    fish
1 coconut
6 slices garlic
2 tbsp poppy seeds
1 tbsp coriander seeds
6 curry leaves

6 red chillies
1 tsp cummin
3 onions
1 tbsp sesame seeds
1 dsp salt
juice of 2 lemons

Cut pomfret in pieces, or fillet them, apply salt and keep aside.

Grate coconut and grind with all the above ingredients to a fine paste. If the paste is not ground fine, strain it.

Heat ½ cup oil and fry finely chopped onions to golden brown, then add the ground masala and curry leaves, fry well until the oil separates, add salt and 2 cups water and bring to a boil, simmer for 30 min., then add fish and some split green chillies, and cook until the fish is done. Add lemon juice and serve.

Will serve six to eight people.

GOA PRAWN CURRY

2 cups cleaned prawns
2 onions
8 slices garlic
1 dsp coriander seeds
¼ cup oil

1 coconut
8 Goa chillies
1 dsp cummin
1 dsp salt
1 tsp turmeric

Grate coconut and grind to a paste with garlic, chillies, coriander seeds, cummin and turmeric; add two cups water to the ground masala and strain it through a strainer.

Cut onions into rings. Heat oil in a pan and add the strained masala, then add raw onion rings and bring to a boil; then simmer for about 15 min. and then add prawns and salt, cook for another 15 min. or to the required thickness. This curry must not be thick.

Add a little tamarind pulp after the prawns are added.

Will serve six to eight people.

MOGLAI CURRY

1 chicken
12 slices garlic
6 cloves
1 piece cinnamon
1½ coconuts
2 tbsp roasted channa
½ tsp fenugreek
½ nutmeg
1 small tin tomato puree
juice of 3 lemons
4 onions

1 piece ginger
6 cardamoms
1 tsp cummin
1 tbsp roasted peanuts
1 dsp coriander seeds
20 red chillies
15 curry leaves
½ tsp saffron
1 dsp sugar
1 dsp salt

Cut chicken into pieces add 4 cups of water, salt and
a piece of ginger and boil until tender, leaving 1 cup
stock.

Extract 2 cups thick milk from 1 coconut.

Grate ½ coconut and grind to a fine paste with garlic,
cummin, cardamoms, cloves, cinnamon, peanuts, gram,
coriander, fenugreek, chillies and nutmeg.

Chop onions finely and fry golden in 4 tbsp oil, then
add the ground masala and fry until the oil separates; a
little more oil may be needed. Then add the coconut milk
and the chicken stock, bring to a boil and let it simmer
for ½ hour, then add chicken pieces, tomato puree, sugar,
lemon juice and saffron (slightly roasted and crushed).
Simmer on slow fire until thick and the oil floats on top.

Will serve six to eight people.

WHITE CHICKEN CURRY

1 chicken
12 green chillies
2 tbsp poppy seeds
1 bunch coriander
1 coconut
1 tsp cummin
2 onions
2 tbsp roasted rice

6 curry leaves
1 tsp chilli powder
2 tbsp peanuts or
cashew nuts
6 slices garlic
1 tbsp coriander seeds
1 dsp salt
juice of 2 lemons

Parboil chicken with a piece of ginger and leave 2 cups stock.

Grate coconut and make 3 parts, extract 2 cups milk from two parts. With one part of coconut, grind chillies, rice, poppyseeds, peanuts, garlic, cummin, coriander and onions.

Melt ½ cup oil, and fry the ground masala lightly on a slow fire add curry leaves, and slit green chillies, if liked; do not brown; then add coconut milk, chicken stock, salt and chicken pieces, simmer until chicken is cooked and oil floats on top, add lemon juice and 1 tbsp of coriander leaves.

Will serve six to eight people.

ARVI LEAVES DAL

1 cup tur dal	6 arvi leaves
1 bunch coriander	8 green chillies
3 onions	1 piece ginger
8 slices garlic	8 mint leaves
2 dsp dhanajeera	1 tsp turmeric
1 tsp chilli powder	½ coconut
1 small piece red pum-kin	2 raw mangoes or 1 tbsp tamarind
1 tsp jeera	½ cup oil

Wash the dal and soak for an hour, then drain; add 4 cups of water and salt and pumpkin cut into small pieces.

Wash arvi leaves, remove the centre stem and chop finely, add to the dal and cook until soft and mushy, strain through a collander.

Grate the coconut and grind with coriander, chillies, ginger, garlic, jeera, mint leaves and mangoes (if using tamarind, soak it in ½ cup water and grind with the masala).

Chop onions and fry in oil until brown, then add the ground masala with dhanajeera, chilli powder, turmeric and fry well. Then add the strained dal, bring to a boil and then simmer to the required thickness. Serve with white boiled rice, fried Bombay ducks, sour lime, chutney, popadums and onion salad (katchumber).

Will serve six to eight people.

MASALA DAL

2 cups tur dal	¼ cup tamarind
¼ kilo red pumpkin	1 kilo red ripe tomatoes
6 red chillies	4 large onions
½ cup mint leaves	6 green chillies
(foodina)	1 bunch coriander
2 dsp dhanajeera powder	12 slices garlic
1 piece ginger	1 tsp turmeric
6 cardamoms	6 cloves
1 piece cinnamon	1 tsp coriander seeds
12 peppercorns	1 tbsp salt
1 tsp cummin	¾ cup oil

Soak dal in water overnight or for at least 2 hours.

Chop tomatoes and cut pumpkin into cubes.

Wash dal, add 4 cups of water, turmeric, salt, tomatoes and pumpkin and cook until soft and mushy, then strain through a collander.

Grind to a paste, red and green chillies, garlic, ginger, cloves, cinnamon, cardamoms, peppercorns, cummin and coriander seeds.

Chop mint leaves and coriander.

Soak tamarind in ½ cup water.

Chop onions finely and fry brown in ¾ cup oil, then add ground masala and dhanajeera, and turmeric and fry well until oil separates, then add the strained dal, and let it cook over slow fire for about 30 minutes, then add mint, coriander and tamarind water.

Cook until the dal is of required consistency. (This dal can be served with tomato rice.)

With mutton added, it will be dhansakh dal to be served with brown rice.

Will serve twelve to fifteen people.

KOILI DAL

1 cup tur dal	2 large bunches
15 green chillies	coriander
1 whole pod garlic	1 dsp cummin
1 piece ginger	8 eggs
¼ cup tamarind	1 dsp salt
8 onions	

Soak dal for an hour, chop 8 chillies and 1 bunch coriander.

Grind one bunch coriander, 7 green chillies, cummin, garlic and ginger.

Chop onions finely and fry in ½ cup oil until golden, then add the ground masala and fry, then add the chopped chillies and coriander.

Cook dal with 1 tsp turmeric and salt until soft, then add it to the above fried masala, and let it simmer until thick, then add tamarind pulp and cook for another 10 minutes.

Just before serving, heat the dal well, beat lightly eggs and mix in the dal, cook until thick. Serve sprinkled with chopped coriander and fried onions. Serve with chapaties.

Will serve eight to twelve people.

COCUM CURRY

100 gm cocum	*¼ kilo jaggery*
2 tbsp rice flour or besan	*1 tbsp dhanajeera powder*
1 dsp salt	*1 tsp pepper*
1 tsp turmeric	*1 piece ginger*
½ pod garlic	*1 large bunch coriander*
6 green chillies	

Wash cocum well and soak in 2 cups of warm water for an hour. Then milch it well and strain the liquid through a strainer, make jaggery in powder and add to the cocum liquid; leave until all the jaggery melts, strain through a very fine strainer.

Grind ginger and garlic, chop onions, chillies and coriander finely. Fry onions in ½ cup oil until golden, then add ginger and garlic paste, fry for a while, then add chopped chillies and coriander, and all the dry spices with flour; fry well, then add cocum liquid and let it simmer over slow fire until oil floats on top.

If liked, 3 tbsp of finely ground coconut can be added. Serve with khichdi.

Will serve six to eight people.

GOR AMLI DHOROO

½ kilo jaggery
½ cup oil
1 tsp salt
½ tsp jeera
½ tsp turmeric
1 tsp dhanajeera powder

½ cup tamarind
2 tbsp besan flour
½ tsp pepper
1 piece ginger
3 large green chillies
½ tsp cummin pounded

Soak tamarind in 2 cups water for an hour, then milch it well and strain through a fine strainer; add powdered jaggery to it and keep until jaggery melts, then strain through a fine strainer.

Chop onions, chillies and coriander very finely. Fry onions in oil until brown, then add all the other masala with the besan and fry well, then add tamarind and liquid and let it boil, then simmer over slow fire until oil floats on top.

If liked, add to it some secta-ni-sing which has been cleaned, cut into pieces and parboiled. Add to the doroo when it is simmering.

This is served with khichdi.

Will serve six to eight people.

BRINJAL BHARAT

1 kilo large seedless
   brinjal
1 bunch green garlic
2 large bunches
   coriander
1 tsp cummin pounded

6 slices garlic
¾ kilo curds
¼ kilo onions
6 large green chillies
1 piece ginger
1 dsp salt

Bake brinjals in a slow oven until soft, or peel the brinjals, cut them into pieces, add enough water to cover and boil until soft, then mash them up completely, if baked, scoop out the pulp and mash well.

Mix the pulp with the curd, slice onions finely and fry in ½ cup oil until brown; then add ginger and garlic paste, fry for a while, then add finely chopped chillies, coriander, cummin and salt, fry and then add the brinjal mixture, cook on slow fire, stir occasionally; cook until oil floats on top. A little sugar may be added, if desired.

Serve with khichdi.

Will serve eight to ten people

SAUCES

Sauces are a treat when used in conjunction with desserts. The right sauce must be used to complement the dessert.

Fruit sauce should be served with plain milk puddings or rich cream puddings. Cream and cream sauce may be served with light sponge and jelly or fresh fruit puddings.

Hard sauce or brandy sauce is best served with rich Christmas puddings.

Rich puddings must be served with plain custard sauce or cream—this also goes for fruit pies.

Plain vanilla icecream served with different sauces make a very grand dessert.

Spicy sauces make very good accompaniment to different varieties of meats.

A good sauce must not be lumpy, it must be smooth when served; so if needed, it should be strained again.

If the sauce has thickened, a little hot water should be added and the same stirred over very low heat until it smoothens and then strained.

SAUCES SWEET

MOCHA SAUCE

2 tsp instant coffee
¼ cup sugar
¼ cup grated chocolate

1 cup hot water
2 egg yolks
¼ tsp vanilla

Mix coffee in hot water. Beat yolks with sugar, gradually add hot coffee to it and stir, add chocolate, cook this over a pan of boiling water, until creamy; add vanilla and serve over icecream.

Rum may be added, if liked.

For vegetarians, omit egg yolks, but mix 1 dsp cornflour mixed with a little cold water, and added to the coffee mixture before cooking.

Will serve six to eight people.

COFFEE SUNDAE SAUCE

1½ cup brown sugar
1 cup water
¼ cup butter
½ tsp vanilla
1 tbsp rum

½ cup sugar
2 tbsp instant coffee
¾ cup evaporated milk or
   light cream
pinch of salt

Combine brown sugar, sugar, pinch of salt, butter and coffee with water, mix well and cook over low heat, stirring until sugar dissolves; then cook until a little dropped in cold water forms a ball (236°F. if you have a sugar thermometer).

Remove from the fire and cool slightly, add evaporated milk or cream and beat well, add vanilla and rum.

Serve warm over vanilla icecream.

COFFEE RUM SAUCE

1 cup sugar
¼ butter cup
pinch of salt
2 tbsp cornflour

1 cup strong black
   coffee
2 tbsp rum

Mix sugar, cornflour and salt in a saucepan, stir in coffee, place over low heat and cook, stirring constantly until it boils clear; add butter, cool and add rum.

Serve over vanilla icecream.

Will serve eight to ten people.

MOCHA RUM SAUCE

2 cups plain chocolate pieces	4 tbsp castor sugar
2 dsp instant coffee	$\frac{1}{2}$ cup hot water
1 tbsp butter	$\frac{1}{2}$ tsp vanilla
3 tbsp rum	pinch of salt

Melt chocolate over hot water, add sugar, coffee and hot water; mix well, add butter and cook until thick; remove from fire and stir in rum. Serve hot or cold.

Will serve twelve to fifteen people.

CHOCOLATE SAUCE—I

2 tbsp cocoa	2 tbsp cornflour
1$\frac{1}{2}$ cups sugar	$\frac{1}{2}$ cup cold water
1 tbsp butter	2 cups hot water
pinch of salt	1 tsp vanilla

Mix cocoa, sugar, cornflour and salt together; gradually add cold water and mix well. Then add hot water and cook over low heat, stirring until thick and comes to a boil. Add butter and cool (if thick, add a little more hot water). Strain through a sieve, add vanilla.

This can be served hot or cold over icecream or any pudding.

If liked add rum or brandy.

Will serve twelve to fifteen people.

CHOCOLATE SAUCE—II

1 cup bitter chocolate pieces	pinch of salt
1 cup water	1 cup sugar
1 cup evaporated milk	$\frac{1}{2}$ cup golden syrup
	1 tsp vanilla

Combine sugar, golden syrup and water and cook to soft ball stage, (236°F if you have a sugar thermometer). Remove from heat, add chocolate pieces and stir until it melts, then gradually add evaporated milk, keep stirring, add vanilla.

If you have no sugar thermometer drop a little of the mixture into cold water and see that it forms a soft ball.

Will serve ten to twelve people.

CHOCOLATE SAUCE—III

2 cups chocolate pieces	½ cup castor sugar
1 cup cream	2 tbsp hot water
pinch of salt	½ tsp vanilla

Melt over hot water chocolate pieces with sugar and 2 tbsp of hot water. Beat until it melts, then gradually add cream and cook for 10 minutes over hot water; add vanilla.

Add rum or Creme de cacao.

Will serve ten to twelve people.

CHOCOLATE SAUCE—IV

1 cup plain chocolate pieces	½ cup water
½ cup castor sugar	¾ cup milk
½ tsp vanilla	2 tbsp butter
1 dsp instant coffee	3 tsp rum
	2 tbsp hot water

Melt chocolate pieces in hot water, add sugar, coffee, salt and milk and stir over low heat until thick and creamy, put it off fire and beat in butter and vanilla; add rum when cool.

Will serve eight to ten people.

CARAMEL WALNUT SAUCE

1½ cups sugar	1 tbsp butter
1 tbsp cornflour	pinch of salt
½ tsp vanilla	¼ cup walnuts
1 cup hot water	

Caramelize sugar with 1 tbsp water in a heavy pan over low heat, until it turns golden brown; remove from heat and slowly stir in hot water, return to heat and simmer for 10 minutes. Mix cornflour and salt with a little cold water and add to the boiling syrup, stir until thick. Cool, add vanilla and ¼ cup chopped walnut and serve over icecream.

Will serve eight to ten people.

CARAMEL SAUCE

1 cup evaporated milk   2 cups brown sugar
2 tbsp butter   ½ tsp vanilla

Combine milk, sugar and butter in a saucepan and stir until sugar dissolves, simmer over low heat until the sauce thickens. Cool, add vanilla and serve over ice-cream.

Will serve ten to twelve people.

BUTTERSCOTCH SAUCE—I

1½ cups brown sugar   ¾ cup golden syrup
½ cup butter   ½ cup thick cream

Place sugar, syrup and butter in a heavy-bottom pan, boil the mixture until it reaches a soft ball stage (234°F). Remove from heat, add cream and mix well. Cool and serve.

Will serve ten to twelve people.

BUTTERSCOTCH SAUCE—II

1 cup brown sugar   ½ cup liquid glucose
1½ cups cream   2 tbsp butter

Combine sugar, glucose and butter in a pan and bring to a boil, simmer over low heat until a soft boil stage (234°) is reached. Remove from heat, stir in cream and beat. If thick, add a little milk.

Serve hot or cold.

Will serve ten to twelve people.

BUTTERSCOTCH SAUCE—III

1 cup brown sugar	½ cup sugar
2 tbsp water	2 tbsp butter

Place all the ingredients in a heavy pan and bring to a boil, simmer for 10 minutes until slightly thick, cool and use.

Will serve eight to ten people.

BRANDY BUTTER CREAM SAUCE

½ cup white butter	1 egg yolk
1½ cups icing sugar	2 dsp rum or brandy

Beat butter and sugar until light and creamy, add egg yolk and beat well; gradually beat in rum or brandy; chill, serve over plum pudding.

Will serve ten to twelve people.

ALMOND CREAM SAUCE

1 cup cream	¼ tsp almond essence
¼ cup finely grated almonds	1 cup icing sugar
	¼ tsp vanilla

Mix all the ingredients and beat until slightly thick. Chill and serve over any puddings.

To make pistachio sauce, add ¼ cup pistachio finely grated, and a few drops of green food colour (omit almonds and almond essence).

Will serve ten to twelve people.

PLUM SAUCE

½ kilo soft plums	2 cups sugar
1 cup water	1 tbsp lemon juice
1 small piece cinnamon	4 cloves
pinch of salt	3 dsp rum

Wash plums, put them in a saucepan, add water, salt, cinnamon and cloves, and boil until they are mushy.

Cool and remove stones. Blend in a blender and strain through a sieve. Add sugar and simmer over low heat until thick; add lemon juice. Cool and add rum.

Serve over icecream, or with any roast meats.

This sauce will stay in the refrigerator for some weeks. If frozen, it will stay longer. If the plums are sweet, add only 1½ cups sugar.

Will serve ten to twelve people.

APPLE SAUCE

6 *soft quality apples*	½ *cup sugar*
3 *cloves*	1 *piece cinnamon*
juice of 1 lemon	1 *tbsp butter*
¼ *cup water*	*pinch of salt*

Peel, core and slice apples, add water, sugar, cloves and cinnamon, and simmer until apples are soft; then remove cloves and cinnamon and blend in a blender; sieve the puree, add butter and lemon juice, pinch of salt, and bring to a boil, keep stirring.

Serve hot or cold with roast pork or duck.

Will serve ten to twelve people.

LEMON CURD SAUCE

½ *cup lemon juice*	1 *tbsp grated lemon*
1½ *cups sugar*	*rind*
3 *eggs*	4 *tbsp butter*

Put butter and sugar on top of a double boiler, stir until butter and sugar blend. Beat eggs well, add strained lemon juice and rind to the eggs. Add this to the butter and sugar mixture and cook over low heat until mixture thickens and coats the back of a spoon, strain the sauce.

Cool and serve over icecream.

It can be used to make lemon tarts.

It will keep in the refrigerator for a few weeks.

CHERRY SAUCE

1 tin cherries (large)
1 tbsp cornflour
1 tbsp lemon juice
½ cup sugar

1 cup cherry syrup from
  the tin
2 tbsp rum

Pit the cherries, keeping them whole.

Mix sugar and cornflour, stir in cherry syrup, bring to boil, stirring well until clear. Remove from fire, add lemon juice and pitted cherries; cool, add rum and serve over icecream.

Will serve eight to ten people.

MADEIRA SAUCE

6 egg yolks
1 tsp lemon rind
½ cup sugar

½ cup Madeira wine or
  rum
¼ cup lemon juice

Beat egg yolks and sugar in the top of a double boiler, add lemon rind, lemon juice and wine and beat all well together. Cook over hot water until it is thick and smooth.

Serve over hot souffles or puddings.

Will serve six to eight people.

ORANGE RAISIN SAUCE

2½ cups orange juice
½ cup sugar
2 tbsp cornflour
1 cup seedless raisins

2 tbsp orange curacao
  or cointrau
1 tbsp orange rind
  finely chopped

Wash raisins and dry, with a clean cloth.

Mix cornflour in a little cold water. Boil the orange juice with sugar, when the sugar melts, stir in cornflour and orange rind, and stir till thick, add raisins and simmer for a few minutes, cool and add liqueur.

Will serve ten to twelve people.

BRANDY CREAM SAUCE—I

2 cups cream
1 cup icing sugar
3 tbsp brandy

1 tbsp lemon juice
1 tsp vanilla

Chill cream, whip until thick (do not overbeat), add sugar, lemon juice and vanilla, mix well, add brandy gradually and mix lightly. Place in a glass bowl and chill.

This sauce is excellent over Christmas pudding.
It can also be frozen and served in squares.
Will serve ten to twelve people.

BRANDY CREAM SAUCE—II

1 cup thick cream
½ cup icing sugar

2 egg yolks
4 tbsp brandy

Beat yolk and sugar until light and creamy, then fold in whipped cream and brandy, chill. Serve over plum pudding.

Will serve ten to twelve people.

LEMON CURD

¼ cup butter
½ cup lemon juice
8 egg yolks

1¾ cups sugar
1 tbsp grated rind of lemon

Beat egg yolks with sugar until light, add lemon juice and rind, and cook in a double boiler, or over hot water, until thick; keep stirring, remove from fire and cool. Stir until the mixture cools, otherwise the skin will come on top. If lumpy, strain through a sieve and fill the jars, keep in the refrigerator.

This can be used for filling tart shells. It can be served on icecream, or applied between two biscuits.

This amount will fill about 24 small tarts.

SAUCES SPICY

MINTY ORANGE SAUCE

½ cup chopped mint
leaves
1 cup boiling water

¾ cup orange shredded
marmalade

Dissolve marmalade in hot water, add mint leaves and leave it to cool. Serve it with any meats.
Will serve six to eight people.

MUSTARD SAUCE—I

1 dsp flour
½ tsp salt
¼ cup vinegar
1 tbsp butter

1 dsp sugar
¾ cup water
2 egg yolks
¼ tsp pepper

Mix flour, mustard sugar, salt, pepper. Add water and vinegar gradually, and mix. Cook all this over hot water or in a double boiler over low heat. Stir until it thickens and comes to a boil, then take it off fire, add egg yolks one at a time and beat well, then add butter.
Strain, if lumpy.
Will serve eight to ten people.

MUSTARD SAUCE—II

3 hard boiled eggs
2 tbsp chopped parsley
½ cup french dressing
½ tsp salt
3 tsp prepared mustard

¼ cup finely chopped
spring onions
1 tbsp lemon juice
¼ tsp pepper

Chop egg whites finely.
Press the yolk through a sieve; to this add french dressing and lemon juice gradually, beat well then add all the other ingredients, mix well; lastly add egg whites and serve.
This can be used as a salad dressing or served with

fish or chicken. More mustard may be added if more zip is needed.

Will serve eight to ten people.

BUTTER SAUCE FOR FISH

Cream half cup butter with a pinch of salt, add pepper, 1 dsp parsley (chopped) and 1 tsp lemon juice. Serve over baked or boiled fish.

* * *

Melt half cup butter in a pan with a pinch of salt and pepper until golden, remove from fire and add 1 dsp of chopped parsley and 1 tbsp of lemon juice. Pour over grilled or boiled fish and serve.

* * *

Melt half cup butter and when it is golden, add to it ¼ tsp salt and ¼ tsp pepper, 1 tbsp chopped parsley, 1 tbsp lemon juice and 1 dsp vinegar and 1 dsp W. sauce; boil all this once and pour over fried fish.

* * *

Melt ¼ cup butter, stir in 1 dsp Anchovy paste and ¼ tsp cayenne pepper. Heat and serve with fried or grilled fish.

MAYONNAISE SAUCE (MADE IN A LIQUIDIZER)

2 large eggs
½ tsp salt
1 dsp sugar
½ bottle salad oil

2 tbsp of vinegar or juice of 2 lemons
¼ tsp pepper
1 dsp mustard powder

Put eggs, salt, pepper, mustard powder and sugar in the liquidizer, run for a minute, then gradually pour salad oil from the top in a steady stream, until all the oil is used up and the mixture is thick. Then add lemon juice or vinegar, mix well; then remove in a bowl, and add 1 tsp of very hot water and mix.

By adding hot water, the oily taste of the mayonnaise disappears and this mayonnaise will keep for over a month in the refrigerator.

Makes 2 cups.

TARTAR SAUCE

1 cup mayonnaise
¼ cup chopped pickle or
  gherkins
¼ cup finely chopped
  cucumber (only the
  hard portion to be
  used)

1 tbsp lemon juice
1 dsp chopped parsley
a few chopped olives
½ cup finely chopped
  spring onions

Mix all the above ingredients together and serve with
fried fish fillets. Pinch of cayenne or a few drops of
tobasco may be used.
Will serve six to eight people.

EMERALD SAUCE

1 cup mayonnaise
1 tbsp finely chopped
  chives
2 tbsp water cress
salt
1 tbsp cider vinegar

2 tbsp finely chopped
  parsley
1 dsp chopped green
  onions
a few drops of green
  food colour

Blend all the above ingredients together in a blender,
strain through a sieve, add food colour and serve over
cold fish or shell fish.
Will serve six to eight people.

CUCUMBER SAUCE

1 cup chopped and
  drained cucumber
  (do not use the
  soft centre)
½ cup mayonnaise
½ tsp mustard powder

2 tsp lemon juice
¼ tsp salt
½ cup cream
pinch of cayenne
a few drops of tobasco
¼ tsp pepper

Mix all the above ingredients and serve with fish or
prawns.
Will serve six to eight people.

SAUCE HOLLANDAISE

This sauce must be made in a double boiler or over hot water.

Beat ½ cup butter with ½ tsp salt and pinch of pepper add 3 egg yolks and beat well; then add lemon juice. Just before serving, add ½ cup boiling water a little at a time, stirring well.

Place the pan over boiling water and stir rapidly until sauce thickens. Serve over fish.

BASIC FRENCH DRESSING

1 cup salad oil	¼ cup vinegar
2 tsp sugar	½ tsp salt and pepper
½ tsp mustard powder.	each

Put all the above ingredients in a bottle and shake it vigorously, or mix in a bowl and beat with a rotary beater, or blend in a blender.

SAUCE VINAIGRETTE

½ cup vinegar	¼ tsp salt and pepper
1 tbsp salad oil	each

Shake all in a bottle or blend in a blender.
Good served with asparagus.

MUSTARD DRESSING

1 cup salad oil	1 tsp pepper
1 tsp paprika	1 tsp horse-radish
2 tbsp prepared mustard	(grated)
(made in vinegar)	2 tsp sugar
1 tsp salt	1 tbsp chopped parsley
¼ cup vinegar	

Blend all the ingredients except parsley. Just before serving, mix in parsley.

BREAD SAUCE

1 cup milk
¼ cup cream
2 tbsp fresh bread
  crumbs

1 small onion
1 tbsp butter
1 clove, salt and pepper

Stick the clove in the onion and boil milk with it, then add breadcrumbs and simmer until thick; remove the onion, add the remaining ingredients and serve hot.
Served with turkey or goose.
Makes 1½ cup.

CURRY SAUCE

2 cups white sauce
1 dsp curry powder
salt

1 onion finely chopped
1 tbsp butter
1 tbsp lemon juice

Melt butter and fry onion until golden, then add curry powder and fry for a while; add white sauce and stir well, give it one boil and serve with fish or chicken. Add one tbsp of lemon juice before serving.
Makes 2 cups.

OLIVE AND PIMENTO SAUCE

2 cups white sauce
1 tsp lemon juice
½ tsp tobasco

½ cup chopped olives
  (stuffed) or pimentos
1 tsp W. sauce

Add all ingredients to the white sauce, heat before serving.
Good with fish or boiled chicken.
Makes 2 cups.

BASIC WHITE SAUCE

2 tbsp butter
2 cups milk

2 tbsp flour
salt and pepper

Boil the milk just before making sauce and keep it hot.

Melt butter, add flour and fry a little over low heat; do not brown, take the pan off fire and add hot milk gradually and stir well, do not make it lumpy. When all the milk is used up and the mixture is smooth, put the pan over low heat and stir continuously until the sauce comes to a boil.

Makes 2 cups.

CHEESE SAUCE

To the above sauce, add 1 cup grated cheese, 1 tsp mustard powder, pinch of cayenne pepper and stir over low heat until cheese melts and the sauce is smooth.

If the above two sauces get lumpy, strain through a sieve before using.

VELOUTE SAUCE

¼ cup butter
2 cups chicken stock
salt and pepper

¼ cup flour
½ tsp grated nutmeg

Melt butter, add flour and fry for a while over low heat, do not brown it, remove from heat, then gradually add hot chicken stock, keep stirring until smooth, return to heat and stir until it boils, add seasonings. Serve over boiled chicken. Add some sherry, if preferred.

Makes 2½ cups.

EGG SAUCE

½ cup butter
2 cups milk
1 tsp mustard powder
1 tbsp chopped olives or
    gherkins

½ cup flour
4 hardboiled eggs
1 tbsp chopped parsley
¼ tsp pepper
salt

Melt butter, stir in flour, salt, pepper and mustard, stir until blended, remove from heat, slowly add in hot milk, keep stirring, cook over low heat until thick and smooth. Add chopped eggs, parsley and olives or gherkins.

Serve with fish or with any vegetables.

Makes 2½ cups.

SOUR CREAM SAUCE

1 cup sour cream
1 cup finely chopped
celery
2 tbsp lemon juice

2 tbsp finely chopped
parsley
a few drops tobasco
salt, pepper

Whip sour cream, lemon juice, salt, pepper and tobasco, add parsley and chill. Just before serving, add celery.

Serve with hot or cold fish. It can also be served over hardboiled eggs or boiled vegetables.

Makes 2 cups.

BASIC BROWN SAUCE

2 kilos veal or beef shin
bones (cracked into
pieces)
1 cup chopped celery
½ cup chopped onions
1 tsp thyme
6 slices garlic
1 tbsp salt
½ cup flour

1½ cups tomato puree
1 cup chopped carrots
6 bay leaves
1 tsp peppercorns
(crushed)
½ cup chopped leaks
¼ cup chopped parsley
12 cups water

Combine bones with celery. onions, carrots. bay leaves, garlic, pepper and thyme. Place all in a large roasting pan and bake in a hot oven (uncovered) for an hour Then sprinkle flour over it all and bake for another 15 minutes. Then remove it from the oven and transfer it all to a large pan. Add 2 cups water to the roasting pan, cook over low heat until the water boils, scrape the pan. to dissolve all the brown substance sticking to the pan then pour this over the bones with 10 cups of water.

Add leeks, parsley, salt and tomato puree. Boil for over 2 hours or until it boils to 1|3rd its volume.

Keep removing the scum off the top while it is boiling.

When ready, strain through a fine strainer. Bottle and keep in the refrigerator and use when required. It adds flavour to a lot of dishes and can also be used for making gravies.

It can be poured into small paper cups and frozen. It will stay for a long time.

BROWN SAUCE

¼ cup butter	1 cup stock (mutton,
2 tbsp flour	beef or chicken)
1 tbsp W. sauce	salt, pepper and cayenne
1 onion finely chopped	

Melt butter add onion and fry until brown; then add flour and brown well, stir in hot stock, stir and cook the sauce until it is smooth and boiling. Strain and serve.

Use whenever brown gravy is needed.

Makes 1½ cup.

ONION SAUCE FOR STEAK

½ kilo white onions	salt, pepper, pinch of
sliced finely	cayenne
½ cup butter	1 tbsp W. sauce

Saute onions in butter until soft, do not brown; season with salt, freshly ground pepper, cayenne and W. sauce. Add ¼ cup hot water and boil for a few minutes. Pour over steak just before serving.

Will serve six people.

ONION SAUCE FOR VEGETABLES

2 cups chopped onions	1½ cups milk
2 egg yolks	1 tbsp flour
salt, pepper	½ tsp chilli powder
1 tbsp W. sauce	2 tbsp chopped coriander

Add onions to the milk and simmer until onions are
tender, remove from fire and blend in a blender, strain.

Beat yolks with flour and add to the onion mixture
with all the seasonings. Cook over low heat, until thick.
Add coriander and serve over vegetables. If liked, coriander may be omitted.

Will serve six to eight people.

SHERRY WINE SAUCE

2 tbs butter
1½ cups chicken stock
¼ cup sherry

2 tbsp flour
2 bay leaves
salt

Melt butter add flour, fry for a while, then add bay
leaves and stock, simmer for a few minutes, stirring until
thick; strain, add sherry and serve.

This sauce goes well with ham.

Makes 2 cups.

ORANGE SAUCE FOR POULTRY OR GAME

½ cup butter
1½ cup stock (mutton,
    beef or chicken)
¼ cup sherry or rum

½ cup flour
1 tbsp grated orange rind
¾ cup orange juice
salt, pinch of pepper

Melt butter add flour and brown a little, stir in hot
stock and seasonings, stir until it comes to a boil. If
lumpy, strain.

Just before serving, add orange rind and orange juice,
bring to a boil, remove from fire, add sherry or rum
and serve.

Makes 2½ cups.

RED CURRANT AND ORANGE SAUCE

1 cup red currant jelly
1 tbsp grated orange
    rind
½ tsp ginger powder
1 tbsp cornflour

1 cup orange juice
1 tsp mustard powder
2 tbsp cider vinegar
salt

Mix jelly, orange juice, orange rind and seasonings, bring to a boil and simmer until all the jelly melts. Mix cornflour with vinegar and add to the boiling mixture. Stir until thick. Serve with any cold meats.

Makes 2 cups.

RAISIN RUM SAUCE FOR HAM

½ cup raisins
½ cup brown sugar
1 tsp mustard
2 tbsp rum

1½ cups water
1 tbsp cornflour
¼ cup cider vinegar
salt, pinch of pepper

Wash raisins, add 1½ cups water and simmer over low heat for 15 min.

Mix sugar, salt, pepper, mustard and cornflour with vinegar and add to the raisin mixture, stir and cook over low heat until thick, add rum and serve.

This goes well with hot or cold sliced ham, or whole baked ham.

Makes 2 cups.

POULET SAUCE

2 cups chicken stock
2 tbsp flour
1 tbsp chopped onion
2 egg yolks
2 tbsp sherry
2 tbsp butter

1 dsp lemon juice
2 tbsp chopped celery
1 tbsp parsley
salt, pepper, pinch of cayenne

Put chicken stock, onion, celery, parsley, butter and seasonings in a saucepan and simmer for 5 min.

Beat egg yolks until creamy, add flour and beat well to this add ¼ cup cold chicken stock, mix well, then pour the hot stock over the yolk mixture, stir well then cook over low heat until thick and smooth; do not boil. Just before serving, heat, then add lemon juice and sherry.

Serve over chicken souffle or sauted sweetbreads.

Makes 2½ cups.

BARBECUE SAUCE

1 cup tomato ketchup	¼ cup chilli sauce
½ cup brown sugar	1 tsp mustard powder
¼ cup vinegar	½ tsp pepper
1 tsp salt	½ tsp chilli powder
2 tbsp W. sauce	2 tbsp butter

Mix the above ingredients together and simmer for 10 min.

To the above sauce you may add 1 finely chopped onion and a few slices of garlic, both fried in a little butter.

To vary the flavour, add ½ tsp of cinnamon or cloves. Chilli sauce may be adjusted to taste.

This sauce is good served with roast beef, mutton or chicken.

It can also be used to baste chicken whilst cooking.
Makes 2 cups.

PIMENTO SAUCE

1 cup mayonnaise	2 tbsp tomato ketchup
1 dsp lemon juice	½ cup chopped pimento
½ tsp cayenne pepper	1 dsp W. sauce

Combine all the ingredients, chill and serve with any cold meats, fish or tongue.
Makes 1¼ cup.

PIMENTO RELISH

½ cup sliced pimento	2 tbsp salad oil
¼ cup cider vinegar	2 tsp sugar
½ cup sliced spring onions	salt, pepper

Mix all and chill.
Serve with any cold meats, chicken or fish.

CAPSICUM RELISH

½ cup chopped capsicum
¼ cup tomato ketchup
salt, pepper

½ cup chopped spring
onion
¼ cup chilli sauce

Mix all, chill and serve.

SALAD CREAM

2 tbsp margarine
2 cups milk
2 tsp made mustard
½ tsp pepper
¼ tsp cayenne pepper

2 tbsp flour
½ cup vinegar
1 tsp salt
2 tsp sugar

Melt margarine, add flour fry a little, take it off fire and gradually add hot milk. Stir over low heat until it comes to a boil, cook for another 5 min.

Let the sauce cool a little, then add mustard, salt, pepper, sugar, cayenne and vinegar. Beat all well or blend in a blender.

Store in a glass jar (covered) in the refrigerator. It will keep for a few days.

Makes 2 cups.

FRUITY CREAM DRESSING

¾ cup orange juice
2 tbsp flour
1 tsp mustard powder
¼ cup vinegar
2 egg yolks
½ cup pineapple juice

2 tbsp sugar
1 tbsp butter
½ cup thick cream
1 tsp salt, pinch of
cayenne

Mix flour, salt, mustard, sugar and cayenne together. Beat egg yolks and beat in flour mixture with the fruit juices, then cook over hot water until thick and smooth. Add vinegar and butter, mix well and cool. Add cream and chill.

This dressing can be used over mixed fruits or mixed vegetable salad.

Makes 2 cups.

KETCHUP DRESSING

½ cup salad oil
1 tbsp sugar
¼ cup vinegar
¼ tsp chilli powder
½ cup tomato ketchup

2 tbsp finely chopped
onion
½ tsp salt and pepper
each
2 tbsp W. sauce

Mix all and blend in a blender, until creamy.
Serve over plain or mixed green salad.
Makes 1½ cup.

CELERY DRESSING

1 cup salad oil
¼ cup sugar
½ tsp salt
2 tbsp finely chopped
spring onion

¼ cup vinegar
½ cup tomato ketchup
1 tbsp W. sauce
½ cup finely chopped
fresh celery

Mix all except celery and beat or blend in a blender.
Just before using add celery.
Makes 2½ cups.

COCKTAIL SAUCE

1 cup mayonnaise
1 dsp W. sauce

¼ cup tomato ketchup
a few drops of tobasco

Mix all and serve with seafoods or fried frog legs.
Makes 1¼ cup.

DESSERTS

A good dessert must be carefully prepared.
*Use the right ingredients — milk, cream and
eggs must be fresh.*

*Essences and colourings must be used very
sparingly, too much might spoil the flavour and
the appearance of the dessert.*

*When using gelatine, always sprinkle it over
a little cold water, let it stand for a while, then
melt it over hot water, until syrupy.*

*Egg yolks and sugar must be beaten at medium
speed in an electric mixer or with wooden spoon
if beaten by hand.*

*Egg whites should be whipped at high speed
in an electric mixer, or with a rotary beater if
by hand.*

*Cream must be whipped very slowly with a
rotary beater to the required consistency, as too
much beating will make it buttery.*

*Custard sauces must be prepared in a double
boiler or over boiling water, over very low heat;
they must be stirred constantly and must not be*

allowed to boil, as they will curdle. If this hap-
pens, they should be taken off fire and beaten
with the rotary beater until smooth, then strain-
ed. There should be no lumps left as that will
destroy the appearance of the dessert.

The custard should be cooled by stirring con-
stantly, otherwise the skin will form on the top
and it will be lumpy again. When cool, it should
be covered with a clean cloth and kept in the
refrigerator.

For steaming puddings, the mould should be
filled only 2/3rds, then placed on a trivet in a
pan of boiling water, which is half way to the
mould; then pan should be closed and the water
allowed to boil; after that the heat should be
reduced and allowed to simmer for the rest of
the time.

The pudding basin must have a tight-fitting
lid, or be covered with a foil.

Be careful when adding liqueur or spirits to
the desserts. Too much of it will spoil the flav-
our, and sometimes even curdle the desserts,
especially fruit desserts and whips in which
cream is used.

RUM CREAM

2 cups milk	6 eggs
½ cup castor sugar	½ cup water
1 cup cream	3 tbsp gelatine
¼ cup rum	½ tsp vanilla

Soak gelatine in ½ cup water.

Separate yolks from whites. Beat yolks and sugar until thick and creamy; to this add warm milk and cook this over hot water until it is thick, do not boil. Remove from fire and add gelatine, stir until gelatine melts; cool the mixture, then stir it on ice or put it in the refrigerator until half set; add rum and cream, beat egg whites stiffly, add ½ cup castor sugar and beat stiff. Fold this in the rum mixture, pour in a mould and set firm. Unmould and serve with any fruit sauce or with some cream.

Will serve six to eight people.

APPLESAUCE FLUFF

1 cup applesauce	1 pkt lemon jelly
1½ cups hot water	1 tsp lemon juice
1 tsp grated lemon rind	1 tbsp sugar
1 egg white	

Melt jelly in hot water, add lemon juice and rind and set on ice until slightly thickened; then beat with a rotary beater until fluffy; fold in applesauce and castor sugar, beat egg white stiffly and fold in the lemon mixture. Pour in a glass dish, garnish with walnuts and glace cherries. Serve with custard sauce or whipped cream.

Will serve six to eight people.

COFFEE CREAM BRULEE

2 cups milk	½ cup cream
3 eggs	2 tbsp sugar
2 tbsp sherry or rum	

Boil milk with sugar and cool, beat eggs lightly and add to the cooled milk, add rum or sherry. Pour the mixture in a well buttered pie dish, put in a moderate oven until well set and brown on top. Pour the coffee syrup over it and put under a griller to caramelize the top. Serve either hot or cold.

Coffee Syrup:

1 cup castor sugar   3 tbsp water
2 dsp instant coffee

Mix all the above ingredients and stir over slow heat until all the sugar melts. Boil for a few minutes until the syrup is thick, then pour over the custard.
Will serve six to eight people.

LEMON MERINGUE PIE

Filling:

1x9" baked pastry shell   2 dsp cornflour
1 cup sugar   1 tbsp grated lemon rind
¼ cup lemon juice   1 cup water
3 egg yolks

Mix sugar and cornflour, add water gradually, add lemon juice and rind and cook all over slow fire until thick and boiling. Take it off fire and add one egg yolk at a time, beating well. When all yolks are used up, strain the mixture through a sieve Pour all in a baked pie shell. Cover with meringue and put in a hot oven until the top is golden.

Meringue:

3 egg whites   3 dsp castor sugar

Beat egg whites with a pinch of cream of tartar very stiff, add sugar and beat, then pile on the pie.
Will serve six to eight people.

GOLDEN SYRUP TART

1x9" unbaked pie shell
2 tbsp white bread-
  crumbs
juice of 1 lemon

1½ cups golden syrup
1 egg
2 tbsp raisins

Mix golden syrup, breadcrumbs, lemon juice and raisins.

Beat egg slightly, and mix with the golden syrup mixture. Pour in the unbaked pie shell and bake in a moderate oven until the pie crust is golden. Serve hot with cream or custard sauce.

Will serve six to eight people.

APPLE MINCE PIE

Pastry:

2½ cups flour
¾ cup butter
pinch of salt

2 tbsp castor sugar
1 egg

Sift flour, salt and sugar, rub in butter, add egg and make a dough, add a little water, if needed. Line the pastry in a tart pan or a pie dish. Leave the remaining pastry aside.

Filling:

2 cups applesauce
½ cup chopped walnuts

2 cups mincemeat
1 tbsp rum

Mix all the above ingredients and pour in the pastry lined pan. With the remaining dough, make a trellis on the top, brush the top with a beaten egg. Bake in a moderate oven until the pastry is done, and the top is golden. Serve hot with rum sauce.

Rum Sauce:

1 cup sugar	$\frac{1}{4}$ *wedge of one lemon*
1$\frac{1}{2}$ cups water	$\frac{1}{4}$ *wedge of one orange*

Combine sugar and water and bring to a boil, keep stirring, then add lemon and orange wedges, and boil for 10 minutes or until the syrup is fairly thick; take it off the fire, remove the wedges and strain the syrup, add $\frac{1}{4}$ cup rum and serve hot with pie wedges.

Will serve eight to ten people.

PINEAPPLE MERINGUE PIE

Meringue:

4 egg whites	*pinch of cream of tartar*
1$\frac{1}{2}$ cups castor sugar	$\frac{1}{2}$ *tsp vanilla*
$\frac{1}{4}$ *tsp salt*	

Beat egg whites, cream of tartar and salt until foamy, then gradually add sugar, beat until meringue holds its peaks. Add vanilla and beat well.

Grease a 9″ pie dish with salad oil, pile the meringue in the centre and spread it in the dish, piling higher on the sides. Put the remaining meringue in an icing bag and pipe small stars on the edge of the pie dish. Bake this in a 300°F oven for over an hour or until dry to the touch. Remove from oven and cool.

Filling:

3 cups crushed pineapple	*2 dsp gelatine*
4 egg yolks	*1 tbsp lemon juice*
1 tsp lemon rind	$\frac{1}{2}$ *cup castor sugar*
1$\frac{1}{2}$ cups cream	

Mix pineapple, gelatine and $\frac{1}{4}$ cup sugar and let it stand for 10 minutes.

Beat egg yolks and $\frac{1}{4}$ cup sugar until light and creamy, add to it the pineapple mixture, and cook over low heat until thick, remove from the fire and add rind and lemon juice. Chill until partially set, then fold in whipped cream and pour all this into the baked meringue shell. Chill in the refrigerator overnight, if possible, or until the filling sets.

Decorate with some whipped cream and walnut halves. If crushed pineapple is not available, use a large tin of pineapple, chop it very fine and use with syrup.

Will serve eight to ten people.

SPONGY COFFEE PIE

1x9" sponge cake (it should be only ½" high) line this on a 9" pie plate, soak it all over with rum or sherry.

Filling:

1½ cups milk	cream walnuts and cho-
2 eggs	colate curds for de-
2 dsp instant coffee	corating.
pinch of cream of tartar	½ cup castor sugar
1 tbsp rum	2 tbsp castor sugar

Beat egg yolks and ½ cup sugar until light and creamy, add salt and coffee, stir in warm milk and gelatine (soaked in ¼ cup cold water). Cook all this over low heat until the mixture is thick, do not boil, remove and cool, add vanilla and rum. Chill until partially set. Beat egg whites with cream of tartar until stiff, add 2 tbsp castor sugar and fold this in the coffee mixture with slightly whipped 1 cup cream. Pour all in the sponge lined dish, chill. Decorate with cream, walnuts and chocolate curls.

Will serve six to eight people.

CRUNCHY PINEAPPLE PUDDING

Grease an oblong baking dish with butter, sprinkle ½ cup brown sugar, arrange some glace cherries and walnut halves over it, keep it aside.

Sponge Mixture:

1 large tin pineapple $\frac{3}{4}$ cup butter
   slices   4 eggs
1 cup castor sugar $\frac{1}{2}$ tsp vanilla
2 cups self-raising flour

Drain pineapple from the juice, keep the juice aside, chop pineapple.

Beat butter and sugar until light and creamy, add eggs one at a time and beat well, add a pinch of salt and vanilla. Fold in flour and chopped pineapple. Mix well and pour this in the prepared pan, and spread evenly. Bake in a moderate oven for an hour or when it is done, a fine skewer inserted in the centre comes out clean. Turn on to a serving platter and serve hot with the pineapple sauce or with cream.

Pineapple Sauce:

Mix 2 tsp cornflour with a little pineapple juice (if the juice is not one cup, add water to make one cup). Stir this over low heat until it boils and is thick, add the remaining chopped pineapple and a squeeze of lemon juice. Add rum, if liked, serve hot, separately with pudding.

Will serve eight to ten people.

SHORTCRUST ROLY POLY WITH JAM

$2\frac{1}{2}$ cups flour   1 egg
$\frac{1}{2}$ cup butter or marga-   1 tsp baking powder
   rine   pinch of salt
1 tbsp castor sugar $\frac{1}{2}$ tsp vanilla

Sift flour, baking powder and salt, add sugar. rub in butter, egg and vanilla, make into a pliable dough, add a little milk, if necessary, or a little more flour may be needed.

Roll the dough into a rectangle ½″ thick. Apply over it any jam that is liked. Roll the dough like a roly poly. Put on a greased baking pan seam-side down, glaze with milk, sprinkle over it some castor sugar and bake in a moderate oven for about an hour.

Serve hot with cream or custard sauce.

Will serve eight to ten people.

PEARS IN MELBA SAUCE

1 large tin pears	*1 cup cream*
1 tbsp chopped walnuts	*1 tbsp castor sugar*

Drain the pears completely from the syrup. Whip cream, add sugar and walnuts. Spread the cream mixture on half of the pears, and press two halves together, making it look whole with cream showing on the sides. Place upright, chill. Serve with melba sauce.

Melba Sauce:

½ *tin raspberry jam*	*1 cup hot water*
1 tbsp cornflour	

Mix jam with hot water and let it melt over low heat, then strain through a fine sieve, mix cornflour in a little cold water, add to the sauce; cook over low heat until thick, cool, add brandy or rum and serve with the pears.

Will serve six to eight people.

APRICOTS IN BRANDY

½ *kilo Iranian apricots*	½ *kilo sugar*
4 cups water	*1 cup brandy*

Pour two cups of water over the apricots and leave for 2 hours.

Put sugar with 2 cups water, and let it melt over low heat, do not boil it. Drain the apricots from the water and add to the sugar syrup, bring to a boil and then let it simmer for 20 minutes over low heat, remove and cool.

Add brandy. Pour all this in a glass jar, the syrup must cover the apricots, so, if necessary, add more brandy. Cover the jar.

This may be served with icecream or whipped cream.
Will serve eight to ten people.

TUTTI FRUITY JELLY TRIFLE

1 tin mixed fruit salad
3 cups hot water
8-10 sponge fingers

2 pkts raspberry or any
other flavour jelly

Lay the sponge fingers around a glass dish which has straight sides; if it is shallow, cut the fingers in halves, joining them with any jam to keep in place.

Drain the fruit salad from the syrup, add enough water to make 3 cups, then boil it and add to the 2 pkts, jelly, stir and melt the jelly completely. Chill until partially set, then fold in the fruits, and pour all in the sponge lined dish. Chill until set, serve with cream.

Add two tbsp of rum or brandy if preferred.
Will serve eight to ten people.

BABA AU RHUM

¾ cup butter
4 cups sifted flour
¼ cup sugar
½ tsp salt
½ cup currants

6 eggs
1 tbsp dry yeast
¾ lukewarm water
½ cup finely chopped
mixed peel

Sprinkle yeast over water, mix well, then add sugar, salt, eggs and 2 cups flour, beat until smooth, beat in softened butter, and mix well; add the remaining flour and knead until smooth, add peel and currants. The dough will be stiff.

Grease a 10″ tube pan and place the dough in, cover the pan with a light cloth and keep in a warm place to rise for over an hour or until the dough rises to the top. (The yeast must be fresh or the dough will not rise).

Bake in a preheated oven 400°F for about one hour or until done; the skewer pierced in the centre must come out clean.

When still hot pour the rum syrup over it soaking the baba completely on all sides, do this gradually until all the syrup is soaked in. Cool the baba, then glaze with apricot glaze. Serve with cream.

Rum Syrup:

2 cups sugar	½ lemon sliced thinly,
1 small orange sliced	seeds removed
with peel, seeds	1 cup rum
removed	1½ cups water

Boil sugar and water until sugar melts, add orange and lemon slices, simmer the syrup for about 15 min., remove from fire and strain, add rum and use.

Apricot Glaze:

1 cup apricot jam	2 tsp lemon juice

Melt apricot jam with lemon juice, over low heat. When melted brush the baba all over it.

Will serve fifteen to eighteen people.

CHILLED RICE PUDDING

½ cup rice	3 cups milk
2 tbsp butter	½ cup sugar

Boil 4 cups water in a pan, then sprinkle in washed rice, boil rapidly for 5 min. or parboil them. Drain off water, then add milk, butter and sugar; let all this simmer over low heat, until the rice is well cooked, and the milk is absorbed.

Custard Sauce:

4 egg yolks   2 dsp custard powder
½ cup sugar   3 cups milk
1 tsp vanilla   2 tbsp apricot jam

Beat egg yolks and sugar until light and creamy, add
hot milk gradually to it, then cook over low heat until
thick, then add vanilla and apricot jam.

Soak 1 cup mixed glace fruits chopped in ¼ cup brandy
and leave for a few hours.

Soak 2 tbsp gelatine in ¼ cup cold water, then add to
the hot custard sauce, mix in the rice and the soaked
fruits. Pour in a wet mould and set in the refrigerator.

Unmould on a platter and serve with Melba sauce or
any other fruit sauce.

Will serve ten to twelve people.

BASIC VANILLA ICECREAM

2 lit milk   1 tin condensed milk
2 dsp cornflour   1 tsp vanilla
2 cups cream

Boil milk add condensed milk and simmer over low
heat, until it reduces by a quarter. Mix cornflour with
a little cold milk and add to the boiling milk; keep
stirring until thick and comes to a boil again. Remove
from fire and cool, stir frequently so as not to form a
skin on top. Add vanilla and cream, blend the mixture
in a blender or strain through a sieve and freeze in the
refrigerator or in an icecream churner.

This icecream must be made one day before, for making
any other icecream desserts and kept in the freezer.

Will serve twelve to fifteen people.

LEMONY ICECREAM PIE

Pie Shell:

¼ kilo bourbon biscuits   ¼ cup butter

Crush biscuits, add melted butter and mix well, press this on a greased 10″ pie dish. Chill.

Half of the basic vanilla icecream to be filled in the biscuit-lined dish. Pour lemon sauce over it, and freeze, sprinkle with walnuts and serve in wedges.

Lemon Sauce:

½ cup lemon juice   1 cup sugar
1 tbsp cornflour   ½ cup water
2 egg yolks

Mix sugar and cornflour, add lemon juice and water and mix to a smooth paste, cook over low heat, stir constantly until thick, add yolks one at a time and beat well, give a boil, remove from heat, cool and strain, then pour over the icecream.

Will serve eight to ten people.

CHOCOLATE MARBLE ICECREAM

1 recipe basic vanilla icecream

Chocolate Sauce:

2 cups plain dark   ½ cup chopped toasted
   chocolate   almonds, pistachio
¼ cup icing sugar   or walnuts
3 egg yolks   ½ tsp vanilla
¼ cup butter

Chocolate Crumb Base:

½ kilo bourbon biscuits   ¼ cup melted butter

Crush biscuits mix with melted butter and press in the bottom of a 9″ spring form pan, and chill.

In a saucepan melt chocolate over low heat or over hot water; add butter and stir, take it off fire and beat in the egg yolks one at a time, again place the pan over low heat and stir and cook until it comes to a boil, remove from heat and beat in icing sugar, beat until smooth.

cool, stir in any of the nuts and vanilla. Spoon this
sauce alternately with vanilla icecream, over the prepared
crust. When the mould is full, run a knife once around
in a swirl to give it a marble effect. Cover with foil and
freeze it overnight.

Before serving, remove the rim of the mould, decorate
with cream and sprinkle nuts over it.

It should be served in wedges when served.

A little hot water may be added to the chocolate, if it
is too stiff whilst melting.

Will serve twelve to fifteen people.

BOMB MOCHA

1 basic icecream recipe, make into coffee icecream by
adding 4 tbsp instant coffee dissolved in a little hot water,
and added to the milk when boiling, or coffee essence
may be used.

Add 2 tbsp coffee liqueur before freezing the mixture.

Line a mould with foil, put in ¾ icecream and line the
sides and bottom, keeping a hollow in the centre. Fill
the centre with the pralin cream mixture. Cover the top
with the remaining icecream, cover with foil and freeze
overnight.

Unmould on a platter and decorate with cream and
sprinkle some pralin over it.

Pralin Cream Mixture:

2 cups cream
1 tbsp coffee liqueur
½ tsp vanilla

1 cup crushed pralin
¼ cup icing sugar

Whip cream until it holds a peaks, then fold in pralin,
sugar, and coffee liqueur. Fill in the hollow.

Pralin:

1 cup sugar   ¾ cup any nuts

Place sugar and ¼ cup water in a saucepan and let the
sugar caramelize, cook until dark brown, add nuts, and
pour on a greased plate and let cool completely. Then
crush to a powder.

Will serve twelve to fifteen people.

MERINGUE GLACE

Meringue:

6 egg whites	1 cup chocolate pieces
2 cups castor sugar	1 tsp cream of tartar
Half basic recipe of va-	1 tsp vanilla
nilla icecream	2 cups cream

Beat egg white with cream of tartar and a pinch of salt until stiff, add sugar gradually beating well until stiff peaks are formed, add vanilla. Make 2 x 9" round on a lightly greased baking pan, and bake in a very slow oven until dry.

Mix chocolate pieces with vanilla icecream. Put one round of meringue on a platter and spoon icecream over it, put the other round of meringue over it, press a little. Whip cream with 2 tsp castor sugar and $\frac{1}{2}$ tsp vanilla, and frost the side of the meringue with it; pipe some stars in a ring on the edge of the meringue. Freeze until serving time.

Just before serving, pour $\frac{1}{2}$ cup chocolate sauce in the centre. Sprinkle some grated chocolate over the cream border.

Will serve twelve to fifteen people.

TOASTED COFFEE NUT ICECREAM

1 basic icecream recipe made into coffee icecream (as given for Bomb Mocha).

$\frac{1}{2}$ cup coarsly chopped	1 dsp butter
walnuts	

Saute walnuts in butter until crisp and crunchy.

When the icecream is half done, add the walnuts, and then freeze completely.

Almonds may be used, if preferred.

Will serve twelve to fifteen people.

PISTACHIO CHARLOTTE RUSSE

1 basic recipe of vanilla icecream to which must be added ¼ kilo of blanched, peeled and grated pistachio, and a little of the green food colour, before it is churned or frozen.

10 to 12 sponge fingers   *2 tbsp apricot jam*

Apply a little of the apricot jam round the inside of the 9″ spring form pan. Cut sponge fingers into halves, arrange them round the pan, flat side against the rim, join them with a little jam in between.

Fill the pan with pistachio icecream, cover with foil and freeze overnight. Before serving, decorate the top with cream and sprinkle some chopped pistachio over it. Remove the rim and serve.

Will serve fifteen to eighteen people.

FRUITY ICECREAM BOMB

1 basic vanilla icecream   *½ cup raisins*
½ cup chopped walnuts   *½ cup rum or brandy*
¼ cup chopped crystaliz-   *½ cup chopped cherries*
ed ginger   *glace*
½ cup crushed almond   *½ cup chopped mixed*
macaroons   *peel*

Soak all the above fruits in rum or brandy, except macaroons.

Next day fold all this with crushed macaroons in the vanilla icecream. Turn it all in a foil-lined mould and freeze overnight. Invert on a platter, decorate with some cream and cherries and serve.

If the fruits can be soaked for 3 to 4 days, the flavour is better.

Will serve twelve to fifteen people.

FANTASTIC PEACH BOMB

1 recipe basic vanilla icecream	2 tbsp rum
1 large tin peaches	1 cup thick cream
¼ cup chopped walnuts	2 tbsp icing sugar

Drain peaches from the syrup. Keep a few aside for garnishing and chop the rest in small pieces, mix them with cream walnut, sugar and rum.

Line a mould with foil, put in ¾ of the icecream and line the sides and bottom, keeping a hollow in the centre. Fill the centre with the cream and peaches mixture, cover the top with the remaining icecream, cover with foil and freeze overnight.

Unmould and garnish with peaches and serve.

The above bomb can also be made with tinned cherries.

Will serve twelve to fifteen people.

BOMB TORTONI

1 basic vanilla icecream, made with chopped and toasted nuts and flavoured with coffee or chocolate liqueur.

Pack all this in a foil-lined mould and freeze. When frozen hard, remove from mould and press all over with the mixture of crushed cream cracker biscuits and any of the grated nuts.

About ¼ kilo of any nuts will be required.

Almonds, hazel, cashew or walnuts may be used.

Will serve twelve to fifteen people.

ECLAIRS VERSAILLES

Choux Pastry:

1 cup plain flour	1 cup water
½ cup butter	4 large eggs
¼ tsp salt	

Sift flour, boil water and butter to a fast boil, lower heat and add flour and salt all at once, beat the mixture until the dough leaves the pan, take it off fire and put

P. R.—8

it in a mixing bowl, beat it with a dough hook (if using electric mixer) or beat with a wooden spoon; then add one egg at a time, beating well after addition of each egg. Beat the dough until it looks shiny and smooth; do not underbeat.

Place one tbsp of the mixture on a greased baking sheet, and bake in a preheated oven 400°F until puffed and dry.

Cool them away from draft, otherwise they will collapse. Makes 12 puffs. Fill them with Creme a la buerre, and pour Apricot sauce.

Creme A La Buerre:

4 egg yolks	¾ cup sugar
1 cup milk	1 dsp custard powder
½ cup unsalted butter	½ tsp vanilla

Beat yolk and sugar until light and creamy, add crushed powder and beat well; then add hot milk and cook the mixture over low heat until thick. Cool a little, then beat in soft butter a little at a time, beat well, add vanilla, then strain through a sieve and chill.

Fill the eclairs with the creme. Just before serving, pour apricot sauce over it or serve separately.

Apricot Sauce:

1 cup apricot jam (if desired use ½ cup apricot and ½ cup orange marmalade)	½ cup hot water
	2 tbsp Cointreau, brandy or rum

Add hot water to the jam and melt over low heat; when smooth, strain through a sieve, add any of the liqueurs and pour over the eclairs.

Will serve twelve people.

CREAM ECLAIR WITH MOCHA SAUCE

Make the eclairs as in the previous recipe.
Fill them with walnut cream and serve with Mocha sauce.

Walnut Cream:

2 cups thick cream	½ cup icing sugar
½ tsp vanilla	2 tbsp chopped walnut

Mix all the above ingredients and chill well. Then fill the eclairs.

Mocha Sauce:

2 cups grated plain dark chocolate	1 tbsp butter
	½ cup sugar
¼ cup hot water	½ tsp vanilla
2 tbsp instant coffee	2 tbsp rum

Melt chocolate over hot water, add coffee and hot water, mix well, add butter and beat, add vanilla and rum. Serve over eclairs.
Will serve twelve people.

GATEAU FILLED WITH CHERRIES

Make the choux paste as given in the previous recipe. Shape it in 9″ round on a greased baking sheet, bake in a hot oven. When the pastry sounds hollow and well baked, turn off the oven and let it be in the oven for another 10 minutes to dry. Remove from the oven and cool; split in half, remove any soft portion from inside, fill with the cherry mixture, place the top over it, spread the top with cream, decorate with some whole cherries and walnuts. Serve chilled.

Cherry Filling:

1 large tin cherries	¼ cup orange juice
2 dsp cornflour	¼ cup sugar
2 tbsp rum	2 cups whipped cream
a few walnuts	

Leaving a few whole cherries, pit the rest, mix orange juice and the cherry syrup, mix cornflour with a little syrup, and add to the cherry orange syrup, cook this on slow heat until it boils and is smooth. Stir constantly, then add the pitted cherries, cool and add rum.

Beat cream with 2 tsp castor sugar, ½ tsp vanilla, spread over the gateau; decorate with cherries and walnuts.

This gateau can also be made with peaches. Peach brandy may be added.

Will serve twelve people.

CROQUEMBOUCHE

Make 50 to 60 small eclairs from the basic choux paste.

Make caramel with 1 cup sugar and ½ cup hot water. Put sugar in a pan with 1 tbsp water, let it caramalize on low heat to a golden brown, add hot water (Be careful as it will sizzle). Stir until a thick syrup is made, keep warm in a pan of hot water.

Filling:

2 cups cream or custard cream (thick), 2 tbsp of icing sugar, if using cream.

Fill the puffs with any of the above cream.

Cover a 9″ cardboard with some foil.

Make a circle of about 9 eclairs, then build the pyramid joining the eclairs with the caramel. Chill.

Melt 2 cups of plain dark chocolate with 3 tbsp hot water; add 2 tbsp rum and pour over the pyramid just before serving.

Will serve twelve people.

BAKED CUSTARD PARSEE STYLE

2 lit milk	1 tin condensed milk
6 eggs	6 egg yolks
1 tsp vanilla	½ tsp grated nutmeg and cardamom
2 tbsp chopped pistachio	2 tbsp chopped almonds
1 tbsp charoli	2 dsp custard powder

Boil milk and add condensed milk, then simmer until quarter of the milk is burnt up; then mix custard powder in a little cold milk, and add to the simmering milk; stir all the time and let it boil for 5 minutes then take it off fire and cool, stir frequently or the skin will form on top.

Beat eggs and egg yolks together lightly, then add to the cooled milk, mix well and add vanilla, nutmeg, cardamom and a few drops of rose essence or 2 tbsp of rose water. Pour all this in a greased baking dish, and bake in a hot oven.

After 15 minutes in the oven, sprinkle the top with nuts. Bake until well browned on top and set. Chill before serving.

Will serve twelve to fifteen people.

STEAMED DATE PUDDING

1 cup butter	*1½ cups brown sugar*
3 eggs	*1 cup breadcrumbs*
pinch of salt	*grated rind of one lemon*
2 cups chopped dates	*1 tsp grated nutmeg*
½ cup milk	

Beat butter and sugar until light and creamy, add one egg at a time and beat well, add rind, nutmeg and salt, then fold in breadcrumbs and dates alternately with milk. Make the mixture to a dropping consistency so add a little milk if necessary.

Pour into a well greased mould and put the mould in a pan of hot water and steam the pudding for 2 hours, or until it is cooked. A skewer inserted in the centre should come out clean. When the pudding is done invert it on a platter and serve hot with cream or custard sauce.

Will serve twelve to fifteen people.

STEAMED APPLE PUDDING

3 apples	*½ cup butter or marga-*
½ cup castor sugar	*rine*
3 eggs	*3 tbsp golden syrup*
2 tsp baking powder	*2 cups flour*
2 tbsp raisins	*½ cup milk*
2 tsp cinnamon powder	*½ tsp vanilla*

Grease a pudding basin and put in the golden syrup. Peel and slice the apples.

Cream butter and sugar until light and creamy, add eggs one at a time and beat well after each egg is added, take it off the beater and fold in the sifted flour with baking powder and a pinch of salt alternatingly with milk, add vanilla and put 1|3 of this mixture in the greased basin, lay half the slices of apples over it, sprinkle with half raisins and nutmeg, cover with another layer of the mixture, lay over it the remaining apple slices, sprinkle with remaining raisins and nutmeg, cover with the remaining mixture. Cover the basin with a foil and put in a pan of hot water and steam for about two hours or until a skewer pierced in the centre comes out clean. Unmould on a platter and serve hot with cream or custard sauce.

Make the mixture to a dropping consistency, so a little more milk may be added.

Will serve twelve to fifteen people.

STEAMED GINGERBREAD

1 cup margarine	4 eggs
1 cup brown sugar	4 tbsp golden syrup
2 dsp ground ginger powder	4 cups sifted flour
1 tsp baking powder	2 tbsp chopped mixed peel
2 dsp rum	$\frac{3}{4}$-1 cup milk

Beat margarine and sugar until light and creamy, add golden syrup, ginger powder and vanilla; beat well.

Sift flour, baking powder, and $\frac{1}{4}$ tsp salt. Fold flour, milk and peel alternately to the creamed mixture; add rum.

The mixture must be of a dropping consistency. Pour in a well-greased pudding mould and place in a pan of hot water and steam for about 2 hours. Serve hot with cream or custard sauce.

Will serve twelve to fifteen people.

BAKED GINGERBREAD

1 cup butter
4 tbsp marmalade
1 tsp mixed spice
1 tsp vanilla
1 tsp baking powder
2 dsp ginger powder

4 eggs
1 cup brown sugar
1 tsp nutmeg
3 cups flour
½ cup milk

Beat butter and sugar until light and creamy, add marmalade, ginger powder, spices and nutmeg, beat well.

Sift flour baking powder and a pinch of salt. Fold flour and milk alternately in the creamed mixture. It should be of a dropping consistency (A little more milk may be needed).

Pour the mixture into a greased and lined 8″ x 8″ pan and bake in a moderate oven until a skewer pierced in the centre of the pan comes out clean. Serve hot with cream.

Will serve twelve to fifteen people.

APPLE CARAMEL

12 large apples
* or 1 kilo sliced apples*
5 eggs
¼ cup rum

1 tsp cinnamon
¼ cup sugar
¼ cup melted butter
2 tbsp lemon juice

Fold apple slices with lemon juice, butter, sugar and cinnamon, place in a baking pan and bake for about 30 minutes, or until apples are tender. Cool.

Beat eggs lightly with rum and fold in the apples, put all in a caramelized mould, place in a pan of hot water and bake for about 1½ hours, unmould and serve sprinkled with some chopped walnuts.

Serve hot or cold with whipped cream.

Caramel:

Place ¾ cup sugar in a pan with 2 tbsp of water and let it melt over low heat until its golden brown and the

sugar is completely melted. Just lift the pan and shake
it; do not stir with a spoon.

Take it off fire, pour into the mould and keep turning
the mould until the caramel coats the sides and the bottom evenly. Cool before putting in the apple mixture.
Will serve twelve to fifteen people.

DELICIOUS PEACH DESSERT

1 large tin peaches	1 X 9" spring form pan
1 tin evaporated milk	(loose bottom pan)
2 cups cream	½ cup sugar
3 egg yolks	1 pkt sponge fingers
2 dsp rum or sherry	juice and rind of 1 lemon
1 X 9" sponge cake,	3 dsp gelatine
1" high	¼ cup of any jam

Fit the sponge cake on the bottom of the spring form
pan, sprinkle some rum or sherry over it. Cut sponge
fingers in halves, arrange round the sides of the pan,
fixing them with some jam in between.

Chill evaporated milk well, by placing the tin in the
freezer for some time, then whip with lemon rind and
juice, add sugar and egg yolks and beat well, then add
gelatine which is melted in ¼ cup peach juice, fold in
whipped cream and rum, pour all this in the sponge-
lined mould. Chill until set. Before serving, remove
the rim of the pan and arrange the peach slices on top
in a design, remaining slices can be served around the
dessert.

Serve with melba sauce.
Will serve twelve to eighteen people.

BASIC CREPES RECIPE

2 large eggs	1 dsp salad oil
1 cup milk	1 cup flour
¼ tsp salt	

Beat eggs, salad oil, and salt in a blender, add milk and flour alternately to make a smooth batter. Leave covered for an hour. Then make about 6" round crepes (about 18 to 20). It can be made in larger pans.

Fill the crepes with any of the following fillings and serve.

Chantilly Cream Filling:

1 cup milk	3 egg yolks
2 tbsp sugar	½ cup cream
2 dsp flour	½ tsp vanilla

Heat milk and sugar, beat yolks until light and creamy, beat in flour until smooth, then gradually pour in hot milk and stir smooth, cook over slow fire, keep stirring, give it a boil, take it off fire and cool, stir occasionally, that the skin does not form on top. When cold, add cream, if lumpy beat with a rotary beater and strain through a sieve.

To this chantilly cream, any liqueur may be added, any nuts or fruits or jam may be added. Crepes must be kept warm and filled just before serving. It can be filled, and a damp cloth put over it and the dish kept in a very slow oven, but not for long.

Apple Filling:

3 cups peeled and sliced apples	1 dsp cinnamon powder
½ cup sugar	2 tbsp butter

Put all the above ingredients in a saucepan and cook over low fire, until the apples are soft, take it off fire, cool, add 2 tbsp rum or brandy and 2 tbsp chopped almonds.

Fill the crepes with the above mixture, lay them on a dish sprinkle 2 tbsp brown sugar over and place the dish in a hot oven for 10 minutes. Flambe with rum or brandy before serving.

Chocolate Filling:

1 tin evaporated milk	$\frac{1}{4}$ *cup cocoa*
$\frac{1}{4}$ *cup hot water*	$\frac{3}{4}$ *cup sugar*
2 egg yolks	*2 tbsp custard powder*
$\frac{1}{2}$ *cup cream*	*1 tbsp butter*
2 tbsp rum	$\frac{1}{2}$ *tsp vanilla*

Mix cocoa in hot water. Beat yolks, custard powder and sugar until smooth and creamy. Warm the evaporated milk, add cocoa and pour over the egg yolk mixture, stir smooth and cook over low heat until it is thick, and boils. Remove from fire and stir in butter and vanilla; beat with a rotary beater and strain; add whipped cream and rum.

Fill the crepes with this mixture, sprinkle with grated chocolate and serve. This filling will do for double the basic crepes recipe or it can be kept in the freezer and used later.

PEACHES AND CREAM FILLING

6 large fresh peaches	*2 tbsp castor sugar*
2 tbsp rum	*1 cup cream*

Blanch and skin peaches and cut into small pieces, add sugar and rum, mix and chill.

Just before serving, whip cream and mix with peaches, and fill the crepes.

Tinned peaches can be used. It can also be made with fresh strawberries.

ORANGE FILLING

2 cups cream	*2 tbsp Cointreau or*
$\frac{1}{2}$ *cup orange marmalade*	*Grand Marnier*

Whip cream, add 2 tsp castor sugar, marmalade, and liqueur. Fill the crepes with it, lay on a platter and pour hot orange sauce over it. Serve immediately.

Orange Sauce:

Juice from 6 oranges
1 tbsp cornflour
½ cup orange marmalade

1 dsp grated orange rind
1 tbsp sugar

Mix cornflour in a little orange juice, then add all other ingredients and cook over low heat until it boils.

Pour over the crepes and serve. A little more liqueur may be added to the sauce.

PINEAPPLE AND PISTACHIO FILLING

1 small tin pineapple
½ cup cream
1 tbsp sugar

2 dsp roughly chopped
pistachio
2 dsp kirsh

Drain pineapple from the syrup, chop into small pieces, whip cream and mix with the pineapple, pistachio, sugar and kirsh. Fill the crepes with it and pour pineapple kirsh sauce over it.

Pineapple Kirsh Sauce:

1 cup pineapple juice (if its less add water to make one cup. Mix 1 dsp cornflour in a little juice and mix with the rest of the juice. Cook on slow fire stirring until thick, add 2 dsp kirsh and pour over the crepes.

STRAWBERRY SOUFFLE

3 cups ripe strawberries
1 cup icing sugar
3 tbsp gelatine
½ tsp vanilla
pinch of cream of tartar

1 cup castor sugar
6 eggs
½ cup water
½ kilo cream

Take ripe strawberries, wash them, drain well, then puree in a blender.

Beat egg yolks with castor sugar until light and creamy, add vanilla. Soak gelatine in water, melt over warm

water, then add it to the egg yolk mixture along with
the strawberry puree.

Beat egg whites with cream of tartar until stiff and
glossy, beat in one cup icing sugar gradually, fold this
into the strawberry mixture, fold in whipped cream.

Pour into a prepared souffle dish, which has been col-
lared with paper. Chill overnight, or for the day. Before
serving, remove the collar and press chopped pistachio
nuts on the sides. Decorate the top with some cream,
and place a few sliced strawberries around.

This souffle is very delicate, so decorate the top very
delicately with cream and strawberries.

CARAMEL SOUFFLE

12 egg whites	4 cups fine castor sugar
1 tsp vanilla	pinch of cream of tartar
pinch of salt	½ cup caramel syrup

Beat egg whites with salt and cream of tartar until
very stiff, then gradually beat in 1 tbsp sugar at a time,
keep beating continuously for about 15 minutes, then
pour in caramel syrup, folding well into the beaten whites.

Turn the mixture in a glass baking dish, which has
been lightly greased with some salad oil, put the dish
in a pan of boiling water, and bake in a cool oven (250-
300°F) for about an hour or until set. Cool, and chill
overnight.

Serve with the following custard sauce.

Custard Sauce:

12 egg yolks	1 cup sugar
4 cups milk	2 dsp custard powder
1 tsp vanilla	1 cup cream

Beat yolks and sugar until light and creamy, beat in
cornflour, then gradually add in hot milk, stir all this
over low heat until thick; do not boil, cool; add vanilla
and·whipped cream. If lumpy, beat with a rotary beater
and strain through a sieve. Chill and serve.

Caramel Syrup:

¾ *cup sugar*
¾ *cup hot water*

*a few drops of lemon
juice*

Put sugar in a heavy pan with 2 tbsp water and let it cook until golden, add hot water to it, being careful as it will sizzle, then let it cook until thick and syrupy. It should be ½ cup.

Will serve twelve to fifteen people.

COFFEE SOUFFLE

1 *tbsp gelatine*
½ *cup sugar*
pinch of salt
1 *cup cream*
¼ *tsp vanilla*
¼ *cup water*

4 *tsp instant coffee*
¼ *cup hot water*
2 *tsp grated orange rind*
1 *tbsp rum or coffee
liqueur*

Soak gelatine in cold water, mix coffee, sugar, salt in hot water, add gelatine and stir until it dissolves, add orange rind and vanilla, chill until half set, then add whipped cream and liqueur, pour in a glass bowl, when set garnish with cream and nuts.

Will serve six to eight people.

MOUSSE TUTTI FRUITY

6 *eggs*
1 *cup castor sugar*
1 *dsp lemon juice*
2 *dsp rum*
¼ *cup chopped glace
cherries*
¼ *cup chopped glace
candied peel*
¼ *cup chopped walnuts*
¼ *cup raisins*

¼ *cup chopped crystalliz-
ed ginger*
2 *tbsp chopped pista-
chio, toasted*
2 *tbsp chopped almonds
toasted*
½ *kilo cream*
pinch of salt
½ *tsp vanilla*
pinch of cream of tartar

Soak cherries, peel, ginger and raisins in $\frac{1}{4}$ cup rum overnight.

Toast almonds and pistachio until crisp.

Separate egg whites and yolks. Beat egg yolks with $\frac{1}{2}$ cup sugar until light and creamy; gradually add lemon juice and rum and mix well.

Beat egg whites until stiff, gradually beat in half cup sugar and vanilla, beat until stiff and glossy.

Whip cream until slightly thick, do not make it buttery, add it to the egg yolks mixture with cream, soaked fruits, and nuts fold into the egg white mixture (do not beat). Pour all this into a large serving bowl and freeze overnight in the freezer.

Decorate with cream, cherries and nuts, leave it in the freezer until serving time and serve straight from the freezer. Do not leave it outside, as it melts soon and loses its flavour.

Will serve twelve to fifteen people.

CHOCOLATE MOUSSE—I

4 eggs	400 gm plain chocolate
$\frac{1}{2}$ cup sugar	$\frac{1}{4}$ kilo cream
1 dsp instant coffee	$\frac{1}{2}$ tsp vanilla
2 dsp rum	

Beat egg yolks and sugar until light and creamy.

Melt chocolate over warm water, add coffee and 1 tbsp hot water, and add to the egg yolk mixture, add rum and vanilla. Beat cream stiff and fold in the chocolate mixture. Pour in a serving bowl and freeze.

Decorate with cream and grated chocolate.

2 egg whites stiffly beaten may be folded in the chocolate mixture lightly; this will give a lighter mousse.

Will serve ten to twelve people.

CHOCOLATE MOUSSE—II

400 gm plain chocolate	$\frac{1}{4}$ cup strong black coffee
3 eggs	$\frac{1}{4}$ cup castor sugar
1 tsp vanilla	pinch of salt
2 tbsp rum	

Melt chocolate with hot coffee, beat in egg yolks one at a time and beat well, add rum and vanilla.

Beat egg whites with a pinch of cream of tartar, add sugar gradually and beat until stiff, fold in the chocolate mixture. Pour in a bowl and freeze. Serve with cream or decorate with cream and grated chocolate.

1 tsp of instant coffee with ¼ cup hot water will also do.

Will serve ten to twelve people.

MOULDED CHOCOLATE MOUSSE

400 gm plain chocolate	*1 cup white butter*
2 dsp instant coffee	*1 cup icing sugar*
1 tsp vanilla	*3 eggs*
2 tbsp rum	*¼ tsp salt*

Melt chocolate in a pan with coffee and 2 tbsp hot water in a pan of warm water.

Beat butter and ½ cup icing sugar until light and creamy, beat in egg yolks and melted chocolate.

Beat egg whites stiffly, then beat in ½ cup icing sugar. Fold this in the chocolate mixture. Pour all this in a foil lined mould and freeze. Unmould on a platter, remove foil and decorate with cream and nuts. Serve with more cream or just by itself.

Will serve ten to twelve people.

FROZEN CHOCO NUT MOUSSE

6 eggs	*1 cup plain chocolate*
1 cup castor sugar	*½ tsp vanilla*
2 tbsp rum	*¼ cup small chocolate*
¼ cup chopped walnuts	*pieces*
¼ cup pralin	*pinch of cream of tartar*
½ kilo cream	

Beat egg yolks with ½ cup sugar until light and creamy, add melted chocolate, rum and vanilla, mix well.

Beat egg whites with cream of tartar and ¼ tsp salt until stiff, beat in ½ cup sugar gradually.

Whip cream, not too stiff, fold in the chocolate mixture, then fold this in the beaten egg whites, fold lightly, do

not beat, then fold in walnuts, chocolate pieces and pralin.
Pour into a chilled bowl and freeze it overnight.

Next day decorate with cream and grated chocolate.
Leave in the freezer and serve straight from the freezer;
do not take it out of the freezer.

Will serve twelve to fifteen people.

PARADISE FRUIT MOUSSE

1 tin evaporated milk	juice of one lemon
2 cups whipped cream	grated rind of one lemon
¾ cup castor sugar	1 dsp gelatine
1 tin fruit salad large	2 dsp rum

Chill evaporated milk in the freezer for at least 2
hours.

Pour in a bowl and whip it until thick and creamy,
stir in lemon juice and rind, add sugar gradually and
keep beating until all the sugar is over. Fold in whipped
cream, gelatine and rum. Gelatine must be soaked in ¼
cup fruit juice and melted over hot water.

Drain the fruit from the syrup completely, put it in a
strainer for some time, then add to the cream mixture.
Pour in a glass dish and chill, or serve in individual
glasses.

Serve some sponge fingers with it.

Any other tinned fruit can be used.

Will serve ten to twelve people.

RAWO

1 lit milk	4 tbsp sugar
2 tbsp ghee	½ tsp vanilla
½ tsp grated nutmeg and	1 tbsp almonds
cardamom	1 tbsp raisins
4 dsp semolina	1 cup cream

Heat ghee or oil, add semolina and fry a little, then
gradually add milk and sugar, stir all the time over slow
fire until thick, take it off the fire add vanilla and nutmeg,

cardamom mixture & cream. Pour into a dish and sprinkle fried almonds and raisins.

Serve hot or cold.

Will serve eight to ten people.

EGG RAWO

1 lit milk	*1 cup sugar*
6 eggs	*1 cup semolina*
½ cup grated nutmeg and cardamom	*½ cup butter or ghee*
	½ cup vanilla
½ cup chopped mixed peel	*1 tbsp almonds*
	2 tbsp raisins

Heat butter or ghee add semolina and fry for a while, Beat eggs lightly, add milk; then add this to the fried semolina, keep stirring until thick, do this on a very slow fire; add sugar, when thick, add vanilla, take it off fire and take it out in a dish, sprinkle with fried almond, raisins, nutmeg and cardamom mixture and chopped mixed peel.

Serve hot. This also makes a good dessert.

Will serve eight to twelve people.

ICECREAMS

The icecream mixture should be prepared one day before it is frozen — it makes icecream smoother and improves the flavour.

The mixture should be left in a refrigerator overnight, next day cream should be added and blended in a blender, the essence added and the mixture left to chill, before placing it in the freezer tray or in an icecream churner.

The icecream container should be filled to ¾ as the icecream will expand as it freezes.

The churner must be packed with ice and rock salt in alternate layers.

The churner should be turned first slowly and then rapidly, until it feels stiff to the hand. The lid must be wiped carefully of all the salt before opening the container. The fan may then be removed and the icecream scraped off it. If the icecream is to be kept in the churner the lid should be closed again and fresh ice and salt packed round it again. The whole thing may then be covered with a thick newspaper and a thick cloth wrapped over it. It may be kept this way until needed.

If you have a deep freezer, the icecream may be removed to a pan with a close fitting lid, and placed in the freezer.

Churned icecream has a consistency of its own and is delicious.

Icecream made in freezer trays forms icicles and is never very smooth. It can be improved if stirred frequently whilst being frozen. Just before service it may be beaten with a rotary beater or in an electric mixer.

Bombs are to be frozen in moulds with tight-fitting lids, or covered with a few layers of foil.